EASY SCRAPBOOK
Embellishment

Heidi Schueller

BEADS • FIBERS • PAINT

Contents

Published by Kalmbach Publishing Co., 21027 Crossroads Circle, Waukesha, WI 53186. Distributed to the trade by Watson-Guptill.

Printed in the United States

11 10 09 08 07   1 2 3 4 5

Publisher's Cataloging-in-Publication Data
Prepared by The Donohue Group, Inc.
Schueller, Heidi.
   Easy scrapbook embellishment : beads, fibers, paint / Heidi Schueller.
   p. : ill. ; cm.
   Includes bibliographical references.
   ISBN: 978-0-87116-249-6
1. Scrapbooks–Handbooks, manuals, etc.
2. Photograph albums. 3. Photographs–Conservation and restoration. I. Title.
TR465 .S38 2007
745.593

Introduction   4

Projects
Listed by main embellishment technique

When I scrapbook, I pile on the beads, buttons, jewels, fibers, paint, ribbons – all kinds of embellishments that make my layout more like a work of art, not just a memory book page. I'm fond of calling my layouts a "work of heart," because I truly love putting time, effort, and creativity into each one. With this book, I'm sharing many of my favorite easy embellishment techniques to help you move your scrapbook layouts to a new level.

Inspiration for your next scrapbook page embellishment can come from anywhere! The funky butterfly on my daughter's shirt inspired me to create the design you'll find on p. 60.

You may want to start small, using just a few of my embellishment ideas in your layouts, until you get more confident about adding more. A very busy layout, which I consider more interesting to look at, can work if it's balanced.

I have a graphic design background and have been designing pages and teaching for a long time. By working through these projects, you too can learn principles of good design and develop an eye for what works.

When I teach, many people ask what inspires me. I use my favorite photos and my favorite color combinations. Often I'm inspired by a certain photo I've taken. Or I may see a layout in a magazine or some cute art on a T-shirt or in an ad, and I'm inspired to create something like it. Inspiration is all around us; we just need to figure out how to incorporate it into a layout or project.

I am a resourceful – oftentimes frugal – scrapbooker. I know it can get expensive when you go into a scrapbooking or craft store. That's why I'm suggesting you try to be inventive with materials you have on hand like paper, crafting beads, fibers, and paint – it will save you a little money and make your layouts that much more original. I must admit, however, that even I give in to a scrapbooking shopping spree once in a while. I just set a reasonable limit on my spending and I stick to it.

Sometimes I'm asked about the archival quality of my embellishment. It's true that some materials I use may someday discolor, or the pages I make may deteriorate. I'm not worried whether my scrapbooks last for 100 years. I create because it's an artistic release for me. My family and friends enjoy my pages today – and that makes me smile.

Heidi Schuelle

TOP 5 TOOLS

THE ESSENTIALS

These are the most basic tools you'll need to get started scrapbooking. Because they're so essential, I don't list them in each project. Make sure you have them at hand before beginning!

Paper trimmer
- the larger the better
- built-in ruler so you can measure and cut at the same time
- safe to use and easy to store because it's flat
- blades are replaceable but long-lasting

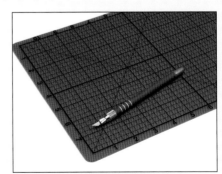

Craft knife and cutting mat
- great for cutting out small items
- use knife to pick up tiny punched dots or to separate tape from a roll
- mat absorbs the cut and has a grid to help measure and line up your work

Embellishment, Heidi-style

Here are a few examples of how I add artistic flair while creating my own easy embellishment.

Chipboard letters come in all sizes, shapes, and colors. But I actually prefer plain ol' gray because I can color it, cover it up, or paint it to match my layout. Buy letters in a style you like (even if they're a terrible color) and cover them to match your page!

Make your own templates for hand-stitched embellishments from a favorite sticker, rub-on, or computer clip art. Put the art on top of the paper you plan to sew and poke holes with a paper piercer or T-pin along the outline of the design through the paper. You'll have a nice pattern to follow with your hand-sewn stitches.

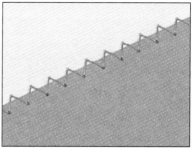

Hand sewing or machine stitching adds extra dimension to pages. I use a zigzag machine stitch to "seam" together two background papers quite often. If you're handy with a sewing machine, this is an easy option that costs next to nothing. When you see "sewing machine" listed as something you need to make the page, that's why.

Stick with it!

BASIC ADHESIVES

This list covers nearly every type of adhesive you'll need for the projects in this book (each project lists the specific type I used). There are many other kinds sold. Feel free to experiment to determine your likes and dislikes.

Runners
My favorite – very easy to use. Runner dispenser applies a thin film of double-sided adhesive. Some are refillable. You even can find runners made specifically for adhering vellum.

Dots
Super-tacky, rubbery dots that come on a backing sheet; apply the dot right where you need it. Available in different sizes and thicknesses. I use the smallest, ultra-thin dots most often.

Foam
This foam has adhesive on both sides. Use it to raise elements off your pages. Various sizes and shapes are available.

Sheets
A sheet of two-sided adhesive allows you to cut any shape and stick one side to your project and the other to beads, glitter, or whatever you want.

Strips
Narrow, high-tack double-sided tape with a backing. Perfect for attaching ribbon.

Clear glaze
Very strong glue-like liquid that dries to a hard, shiny, transparent glaze. Useful for attaching tiny things like jewels or to give a shiny coating to tags.

Super-hold adhesive roll
Very powerful and great for holding metals, fabrics, or even heavier three-dimensional items.

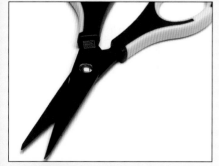

Scrapbooking scissors
- my favorites are coated in Teflon, so adhesive-backed items don't stick
- small, pointy tips get into tight corners of little letters and embellishments
- extremely sharp; cut through most ribbon and fabric smoothly

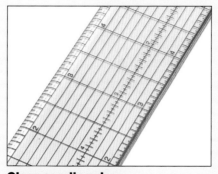

Clear acrylic ruler
- see and count increments under the ruler as you work
- align elements with precision

Hole punches
- "must-have" for putting holes in tags and other paper decorations
- I punch holes in borders to add detail
- a ¼-in. (.6cm) hole punch is good for starters; add others as you progress

Time to scrapbook

I have three young daughters, and I know it can be challenging to find time to create art or work at a hobby, even when you love it. I scrapbook when my youngest takes her afternoon nap and at night when everyone is asleep. You need to set time aside to scrap, just as you would schedule time to see a movie or go to the gym. Tell the family you can't be disturbed for two hours because you need to scrap. Try getting together with a friend or two on a Friday night, pop some popcorn, and set the kids up with a movie while you scrap. Some of us have the luxury of a craft room where scrapping supplies can be left out, ready to use as time permits. If you don't, make up a portable scrap station using a large craft tote that holds everything you need. Pull it out when you have a spare half hour and get a little scrapping done!

7 PRO TOOLS

MAKE LIFE EASIER

Moving right along? Consider adding some of these tools as your skills progress. They help make page construction go faster, so you'll be able to spend more time designing and embellishing!

Circle cutters
These feature a blade that follows a circular template, enabling you to cut circles quickly and precisely. Oval cutters are available, too.

Bead tray and tweezers
A bead tray is great for holding or sorting beads, buttons, or jewels, and it keeps tiny things from rolling off your work surface. Some have a plug that can be removed to return beads to a container. Tweezers are helpful for positioning tiny items on layouts.

Embossing heat tool
This tool heat-sets embossing powder. I use it in several projects in this book. An embossing heat tool isn't expensive, and if you enjoy stamping and card-making as well as scrapbooking, you may find it worthwhile to add to your tool kit.

Craft or jewelry pliers
Using heavy household pliers just won't do! When you need to open a small jump ring or twist thin wire for seed beads, you need small craft pliers.

Foam brushes
You don't have to spend a lot of money on paintbrushes. Inexpensive foam brushes work great. If they get ruined, as when acrylic paint dries on them, it's not a big loss. Just throw them out.

Brayer/roller
This tool applies even pressure as you roll it over an area. It is helpful for pressing beads into adhesive or adhering photos in place without using your fingers, which could leave greasy marks.

Paper piercer
Use this tool to poke holes through paper or cardstock before hand stitching a fiber embellishment. It's easier to hold and stronger than a T-pin. Use a pad underneath to protect your work surface.

Where to store all this stuff?

I keep my fibers in a clear, 2-in. (5cm) tall fishing tackle box. I store ribbon spools on wooden dowels. For storing paper, try clear magazine boxes or big file bins where you can file by color or pattern. Craft stores have lots of styles of divided storage boxes for storing smaller items like beads, buttons, brads, and eyelets.

I keep stickers in a plastic file organizer I bought at an office supply store. It has at least 25 pockets, and I labeled them for small letters, round letters, block letters, rub-ons, etc. It's wide, so even my longer sets of stickers fit nicely.

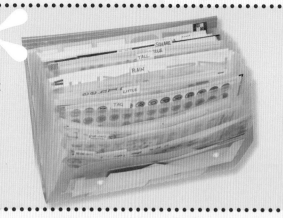

How to use this book

For each scrapbook layout, I focus on one embellishment technique, explaining in detail how it was created. I also call out other embellishments used. It's up to you whether you simply enjoy learning the specific technique or want to "scraplift" the entire layout. If you choose to duplicate the page, a key showing time and expertise for completing the whole project will help you plan.

Featured embellishment technique

Other embellishments used

Step-by-step instructions for featured technique

Micro beads over die cut

letters printed on transparency

WHERE IN THE WORLD IS

CAMPING frog?

9-29,93,94
Schueller

My photo subject was Camping Frog, a multicolor, globe-trotting kind of guy. I found a frog die cut and just needed to add beads for color! With this technique, you simply cut away the adhesive backing bit by bit in order to place beads with a lot of control.

chipboard letters

...for the embellishment
- die cutting machine or die cut frog shape
- cardstock
- double-sided, peel-and-stick adhesive sheet
- craft knife
- micro beads (several colors)
- brayer (optional)

...to make the whole page
- patterned paper
- chipboard letters
- self-adhesive ink jet transparency
- circle cutter
- adhesive (runner)
- computer

time ● ○ ○
expertise ● ○ ○

If you don't have access to a die-cutting machine, trace a pre-die-cut shape and trim with a craft knife.

1 Measure die cut and cut a piece of white cardstock and adhesive sheet a little larger than die cut. Peel backing off one side of adhesive and attach to cardstock. Trim cardstock using a die-cutting machine or by hand.

2 Use a craft knife to cut small segments of adhesive backing from the shape. Peel off the backing and sprinkle one color of beads over exposed area. Press the beads down firmly. (A brayer is helpful for making sure the beads adhere well.)

3 Repeat step 2 with other colors of beads, doing one color at a time until entire shape is filled.

74

Don't forget
- Always have the basic tools at hand
- You'll need your own photos, sized for each layout

Box tells what's needed to create only the featured embellishment technique OR to make the entire layout

"Do I need a computer?"
On many page layouts, I used my computer to set up and print titles and journaling (text). Feel free to add these details by hand.

Key for completing entire scrapbook page

time
● ○ ○ 1-2 hours
● ● ○ 3-4 hours
● ● ● 4+ hours

expertise
● ○ ○ beginner/easy
● ● ○ advanced/moderate
● ● ● skilled/challenging

For more details about the products I used and my sources, see p. 94.

button

French knots

schvellers

By the time we returned home from our refreshing walk, a thousand more leaves had fallen in front of our neighbor's yard. (Our old maple tree doesn't lose its leaves until December!) So the girls helped Julie and Dave rake their leaves into several big piles. We had leaf fights, long jump contests and leaf tackle torture. It was an amazing family day with awesome seasonal photos!

One of the best aspects of living in Wisconsin, is the four changing weather. On this season proposes unpredictable opportunity to experience the fun. Although each to have found ourselves seasons: in which we strive smelling autumn leaves. are usually a few perfect the block and of course we took a stroll around giggling in the crisp, deliciously beautiful fall days in dancing and jumping, leaping, while I ran inside to grab the camera.

2005

Etymology: Middle
from Latin spiritus, li
1: an animating or vital p
2: a su

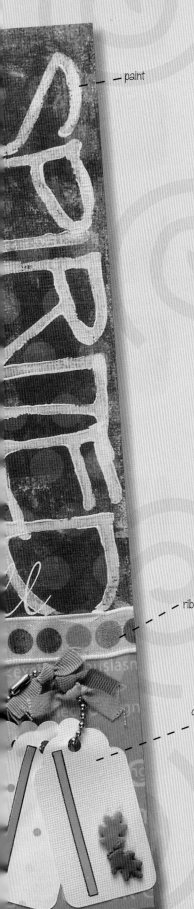

paint

ribbon

die-cut tags
with chain

It's a fantastic fall day! The modeling compound I used for my autumn leaves is super-easy to use and it air dries – no baking. I mixed acrylic paint with the compound before I shaped it, although it's easy to paint after it dries too.

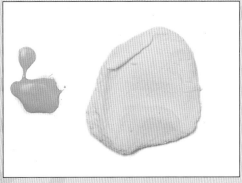

1 Mix a little acrylic paint with modeling compound until you get the color you want.

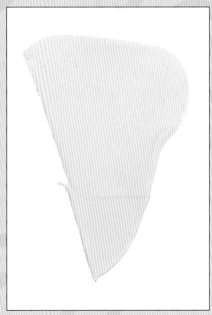

2 Roll the colored compound until it's paper thin. Rolling on a transparency or laminated surface will help release the thin sheet. Let dry for about 30 minutes.

3 Using a leaf punch or die cutter, punch leaf shapes from dry compound. Attach to layout using adhesive dots.

...for the embellishment
- acrylic paint
- Delight modeling compound
- leaf punch

WHAT YOU NEED

...to make the whole page
- patterned paper
- cardstock
- circle cutter
- stickers
- rub-on letters
- die-cut tags
- beaded chain
- lettering template
- ribbon (two styles)
- alphabet stamps
- acrylic paint (yellow, gold, burnt umber, berry, pumpkin)
- sponge brush

- fiber
- button
- paper piercer
- embroidery needle and thread
- adhesives (runner, vellum runner, dots)
- computer
- sewing machine

time ● ● ●
expertise ● ● ○

hemp border

stickers

One of my favorite restaurants to visit when I travel to Appleton is Nauts Landing in Menasha. Or is it in Neenah? I'm never sure. Once we cross over the bridge we enter a series of islands, and I get all twisted up. The restaurant is decorated with a nautical theme and sits on the edge of the river where a variety of boats harbor for the night.

It is amusing to watch the boats while sitting outside on the deck and the food is delicious. Of course, the company isn't all bad either! 6/06

Maybe I should have called this "Knots Landing?"

Knotting is just the right touch for these nautical-theme borders. If you can tie a square knot, you can create borders like mine. (And if you can't, I provide the instructions!) I used hemp. Because knotting, also known as macramé, is so popular in jewelry crafts, you should be able to find a variety of cord for this technique.

...for the embellishment
- glass beads
- hemp cord
- clamp to hold cord

...to make the whole page
- patterned paper
- stickers
- self-adhesive ink-jet transparency
- adhesives (runner, super-hold)
- computer

time ●●○
expertise ●●○

WHAT YOU NEED

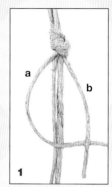
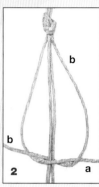

1 Tie four 25-in. (64cm) strings of hemp cord together at one end. Keep two of the strings in the middle of your braid at all times. These two strands will never move; they act as the backbone of the braid. Begin with cord **a** on the left. Lay it over the center two strands and cross **b** over **a**.

2 Cross **b** under **a** and then under the two middle strands. Finish by bringing **b** back up over **a** on the left and pull both tight.

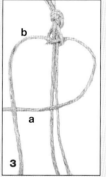
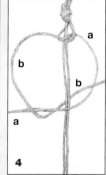

3 For the next knot, cross **a** over the two center strands and then under **b**.

4 Cross **b** under **a** and behind the two center strands. Finish by bringing **b** over **a** and pull both tight. Repeat steps 1 through 4 until you have completed six knots.

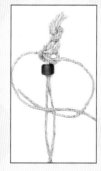

5 To add a bead, slide a bead over the two center strands and then tie a knot as in steps 1 and 2. Add another bead and tie a knot as in steps 3 and 4. Add another bead and continue tying six more knots. Repeat, adding beads until you reach the length of braid you need.

explore

discover

Moments like these are the kinds I will remember forever in my mind. Watching Laurelei learn how to blow dandelions after copying her sister Isabel made me giggle. She put the flower right up to her lips and tried so hard to blow off all the seeds! After most of the seeds blew off, she inspected what was left and picked the last of the seeds off with her fat little fingers. I'm guessing each wish will come true, as I'm sure I'll be digging out lots of weeds next spring!   Laurelei - 2 May 2006

make a

wish

Paper flowers are so sweet. They are easy to find in a range of colors, from pastel to bright. Some will have a hole already punched in the center, but if not, it's easy enough to do with a paper piercer or T-pin. I stitched pearl beads to the center of each flower, creating a soft frame for the photos.

ribbon

chipboard letters

1 Use a paper piercer or a T-pin to make a small hole in the layout and the center of the paper flower (if it doesn't already have a hole).

2 Insert a threaded needle from the back of the layout to the front, going through the flower and a pearl.

3 Finish by inserting the needle back through the same hole. Repeat for all flowers.

...for the embellishment
- pearl beads
- paper flowers
- threaded needle
- paper piercer or T-pin

WHAT YOU NEED

...to make the whole page
- patterned paper
- ribbon
- stickers
- chipboard letters
- circle template
- adhesives (runner, dots)
- computer

time   ● ● ○
expertise   ● ○ ○

Beaded spirals

metal-rimmed tag

backstitched fiber

flower cutouts

Sisters...

Let's take a walk beyond this tree, we'll take it slow just you and me
We'll talk and laugh as sisters do, keeping in mind we're best friends too
This day is special more than we know, your hand in mine we will go
Sooner than later women we'll be, so let's take it slow just you and me

Once you get the hang of making beaded spirals with craft wire and round-nose pliers, you'll find lots of uses for this little accent. After I placed the beaded wire, I outlined and emphasized the shape with hand stitching.

beaded leaves

ribbons

2005

...for the embellishment

- 26-gauge craft wire
- seed beads
- roundnose pliers
- wire cutters

**WHAT YOU
NEED**

...to make the whole page

- cardstock
- patterned paper
- borders and flower templates
- embroidery needle
- fibers
- rub-on letters
- stamps and ink pad
- metal-rimmed tag

- circle punch
- ribbon
- paper piercer or T-pin
- adhesive (runner)
- computer

time   ● ● ●
expertise ● ● ○

1 Cut a 3-in. (7.6cm) piece of 26-gauge craft wire and use round-nose pliers to turn a small loop at one end. String pink seed beads onto the wire, shaping the wire into a spiral as you add beads.

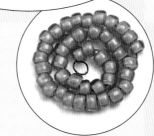

2 When the spiral is large enough to fill the center of the flower, turn a small loop and trim the excess wire. Attach the beaded spiral to the flower center with needle and thread, and adhere the stitched and beaded flowers above the stems.

PATTERN
page
92

WHAT YOU NEED

...for the embellishment
- cardstock
- ink pads
- clear glaze
- small bead tray
- micro beads

...to make the whole page
- patterned paper
- cardstock
- stickers
- alphabet stamps
- ribbon
- rickrack
- letter stamps
- acrylic paint (red, white, pink)
- adhesive (runner)
- computer
- sewing machine

time ● ● ●
expertise ● ● ○

This three-tier ice cream cone can be a lot of fun to make. Vary the paper colors to create your own delicious flavors, then pile on the toppings!

rickrack

RECIPE
for a good Ice Cream Picnic!
Two Gallons of Ice Cream
10 to 12 Toppings
Approx. 350 lbs. of Kids
One Hot Summer Day
A Pinch of Humidity
Bowls & Spoons Optional
3 Boxes Handi-Wipes
Makes Plenty of Smiles

machine stitching

1 Trace and cut out three ice cream scoop shapes and one cone shape from colored cardstock. Ink edges. Using clear glaze, squeeze out little lines or dots onto ice cream shape. (For a shape that will have multiple colored beads, squeeze out just a few dots or lines for the first color).

2 Using a bead tray, sprinkle first color of micro beads (purple) over the glaze. Let dry, tap excess beads off shape, and pour beads back into container.

3 Repeat step 2 for additional colors. Use this technique for each ice cream shape.

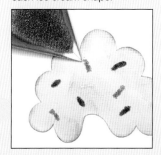

Be creative! Have fun and create lots of cute and colorful toppings for your ice cream scoops. It's OK if they're colors you'd never eat!

100 PERCENT GOOD

99% of TI

GOOD

rickrack

machine stitching

Cinder - March, April, May 2006

raised punched dots

In times past, a hat pin neatly secured a lady's hat. Today you'll find modern versions sold for crafting use. I adorn mine with beads and use them to accent special pages.

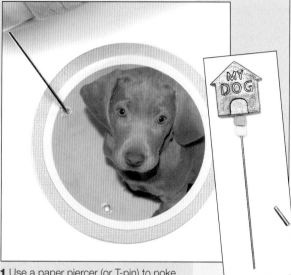

1 Use a paper piercer (or T-pin) to poke two holes through photo and cardstock where pin embellishment will be placed.

2 Slide two or three beads onto embellishment pin all the way to the top.

3 Starting on the front of the layout, carefully push embellishment pin through the top hole to the back side of the layout. Then push the pin back through the bottom hole and up to the front of the layout. Place cover on tip of pin.

stickers

DON'T STOP THERE... I embellished a giant hat pin and used it as part of this cool journal cover.

frame holders

ribbon

French knots and beads make a strong initial letter. Although this technique looks challenging, it's easy to accomplish with a little planning. Brads complete the title.

1 Print out title from computer. Trim with scissors and lay it over the cardstock on your layout where you want the beaded title to be stitched.

2 Using a paper piercer or T-pin, poke holes along the letters in the title. Take into account the size of the beads you intend to sew onto the title; the holes will need to be spaced accordingly.

3 Using embroidery thread and needle, bring the needle up through the back of the cardstock and through the bottom of the bead. Tie a French knot and pull the needle back down through the front of the bead, through the same hole in the cardstock to the back again. Repeat for each bead.

Tip

To help your page slide into your page protector with ease, use tape to cover the bent brad prongs on the back of the layout. The prongs won't get caught on the page protector when you slide it in.

Need a refresher on French knots? Turn to page 93.

...for the embellishment
- computer-printed title
- paper piercer or T-pin
- embroidery needle and thread
- metal flower beads

...to make the whole page
- cardstock
- patterned paper
- die-cut saying
- mini brads
- frame holders
- ribbon
- adhesive (runner, strips)

WHAT YOU NEED

time ●●○
expertise ●●○

Fancy paper clips come in many shapes and sizes. I especially love the spirals. Add beads and they easily become a playful page accent.

...for the embellishment
- decorative paper clips
- beads
- circular slide mounts

...to make the whole page
- patterned paper
- ribbon
- die-cut tag
- rub-ons
- stickers
- mini brads
- adhesive (runner, strips)
- computer
- sewing machine

WHAT YOU NEED

time	●●○
expertise	●○○

1 Choose the appropriate style of clip for this technique based on how easily the bead slides onto and around the paper clip.

2 Slide three beads onto a paper clip and push them as far as needed.

3 After all three beads are in position, push the outside end of the paper clip under the circular slide mount and twist the paper clip until the same end comes completely around and under the slide mount again. This will keep the paper clip flat. (If the outside end of clip is not tucked under twice, the clip will flip upward.)

ribbon

tag

brads

cular slide mounts

machine stitching

baby girl

Happy Birthday

For your six month old party, your sisters and I shared, straight from the can, Reddi Wip Topping! We just all opened wide while I squirted the foamy white stuff into all of our mouths. You didn't quite understand the concept of opening your mouth and just kept grabbing at the can, so I just sprayed some onto your high chair tray. It didn't take long before you started rubbing your hands in it and licking it off the tray. You had it all over your face and then decided to put a glob on top of your head. Your sisters and I giggled and had a great time getting sticky. We had fun celebrating this big day in your life. Half a year old is nothing to snooze over. After we polished off the can, we all headed outside and hosed off in the warm September sun. 9-04

Laurelei

machine
stitching

brads   paper flow

Sure, you can buy chipboard letters in many colors and patterns. But I have more fun painting my own. This is a great example of the results you can get. Grab your acrylic paints and get a little messy!

giant rickrack

DON'T STOP THERE...

To make a key fob, paint a chipboard letter with acrylic paint. To add a patterned paper frame, trace the circle frame and letter outline onto patterned paper. Cut out and adhere to chipboard letter frame. Glue letter back in place and coat with decoupage medium or other clear glaze. Add coordinating ribbon and a ring for your keys.

...for the embellishment
- acrylic paint
- paintbrush
- chipboard letters
- dauber or cotton swab

WHAT YOU NEED

- giant rickrack
- paper flowers
- mini brads
- adhesive (runner, dots, super-hold)
- computer
- sewing machine

...to make the whole page
- cardstock
- patterned paper
- ribbon

time   ● ● ○
expertise   ● ○ ○

1 Using acrylic paints and a small paintbrush, paint chipboard letters and let dry. For the circular chipboard letter, punch out the inside letter and paint the chipboard frame. Paint the inside letter of the chipboard circle a different color and let dry.

2 Using a dauber or a cotton swab, dab the edges of the chipboard letters and circle frame in a contrasting color. When everything is dry, push the chipboard letter back inside the circular frame.

Stamped title letters

mini buttons

machine stitching

Horeb Springs Park

Jan. '06

I love the look of letters that are stamped with acrylic paint. It's a much bolder effect than using an ink pad, and the irregularities in the letter shapes add a lot of personality.

Tip ✳
Stamping with acrylic paint can be slippery. Don't press too hard or the stamp may go sailing off the page! Press just enough to leave a clean impression.

punched snowflakes

1 Use a foam paintbrush to dab paint onto the stamp, covering it completely and smoothly.

2 Carefully place the stamp onto your layout. Apply even pressure for a complete print. Pull off gently and wash the stamp immediately so the acrylic paint doesn't ruin your stamp.

...for the embellishment
- foam brush
- acrylic paint (plum)
- letter stamp

...to make the whole page
- cardstock
- patterned paper
- compass
- letter stickers
- mini buttons
- large and small snowflake punches
- circle punch
- adhesive (runner, dots)
- gel pens (white, black)
- sewing machine

WHAT YOU NEED

time ● ● ○
expertise ● ● ○

My photo suggested a garden theme. I created a soft border of paper flowers connected by a semicircle of beads.

machine stitching

tag   ribbon

chipboard letter with ribbon

gg betty and laurelei

What feeling is so nice as a child's hand in yours.

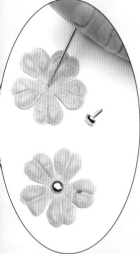

1 Use a paper piercer or T-pin to make a hole through paper flower and layout. Attach mini brads through holes.

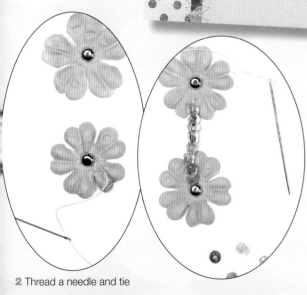

2 Thread a needle and tie opposite end around brad.

3 Slide enough beads onto needle and thread, making a connection to the next brad. Wrap thread tightly but carefully around next brad and continue to repeat step 3 with each brad. Tie a knot around the last brad to finish.

...for the embellishment
- paper flowers
- mini brads
- beads
- paper piercer or T-pin
- threaded needle

WHAT YOU NEED

...to make the whole page
- patterned paper
- ribbon
- chipboard letter
- die-cut tag
- rub-on letters
- lettering template
- brown marker

- compass
- adhesive (runner, foam squares)

time   ● ● ○
expertise   ● ● ○

milwaukee county **ZOO**

April 2006, clauds asks:

"Are We **tough**? yes i s

AND i've got your **nu**

magnets
glued with
foam squares

bubble stickers

Sometimes it's fun to pick a design element in your background paper and repeat it using an embellishment. I had some wood craft rings that nearly matched the size of the circles in my paper. Painted and glued, they add a nice note of repetition to the design.

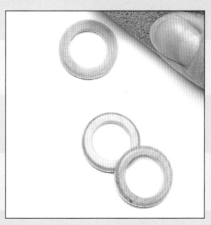

1 Lightly sand the surface of the wooden rings so the paint will adhere to the wood.

2 Paint wooden ring, inside and outside. Let dry. Adhere to layout.

monogram letters

Don't limit your-self to just one font for journal-ing. Try a mix of sticker styles, stamped letters, and rub-ons for an extra-lively page.

WHAT YOU NEED

...for the embellishment
- wood rings
- sandpaper
- acrylic paint
- small paintbrush

...to make the whole page
- patterned paper
- monogram letters
- rub-ons
- ribbon
- phone number magnets
- white block stickers
- bubble letter stickers
- stamps and ink pad

- adhesive (runner, strips, super-hold, foam squares)
- sewing machine

time　　●●○
expertise　●●○

DON'T STOP THERE...

I enhanced a purchased see-through souvenir box with a lot of the same embellishments you see on my scrapbook pages: wood rings, beads, stamped letters, and rub-ons. Now it holds mementos of my travels.

Paris — June 1997

It's not how fast you get there, but how long you stay.
— Patty Berg

ribbon

staples

vellum quote

I created the coins that make up this border. They're easy to do and look great. Look for patterned paper that features a design of an antique map or foreign currency. And consider other arrangements for your coins – they don't have to stay in a rectangle.

...for the embellishment

- patterned paper
- chipboard
- circle punch
- ink pad
- paper piercer or T-pin
- threaded needle
- beads

...to make the whole page

- patterned paper
- vellum quote
- ribbon
- stapler
- adhesive (runner, dots)
- computer

WHAT YOU NEED

time ●○○
expertise ●○○

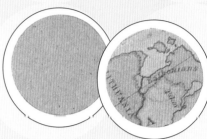

1 Punch circles from patterned paper and chipboard. I used ⅞-in. (2.2cm) and 1-in. (2.5cm) punches, but you can use whatever size you like. Adhere the patterned paper circles to the chipboard circles.

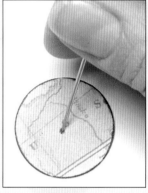

2 Ink the edges of the circle for a distressed look. Use a T-pin or a paper piercer to poke a hole in the center of each.

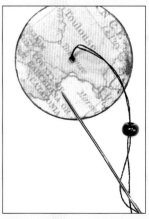

3 Tape the end of a threaded needle to the back of the circle. Pull needle through the hole to the front and slide on a bead. Bring needle back down the same hole in circle and tape the thread end to the back. Cut thread. Repeat, sewing a bead to each circle.

It's pretty clear where I wanted you to look in this photo. Seed-bead circles draw the viewer's eye and add an element of lighthearted repetition to this layout.

...for the embellishment

- seed beads
- small bead tray
- threaded needle
- circle template
- pencil
- clear glaze
- tweezers

 WHAT YOU NEED

...to make the whole page

- cardstock
- patterned paper
- stickers
- buttons
- fiber
- chipboard letters
- lettering template
- black marker
- adhesive (runner, dots, super-hold)
- sewing machine

time ● ● ○
expertise ● ○ ○

photo 6-06

swinging BRINGS OUT THE Kid IN EVERYONE!

buttons   machine stitching   chipboard letters

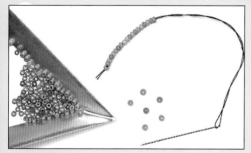

1 Pour seed beads into tray and thread them onto needle and knotted thread.

 Tip

Lids from plastic containers and jars in various sizes are handy substitutes if you don't have a circle template.

2 Trace a circle in pencil (or light pen) using a circle template. Outline the circle with a thin line of clear glaze.

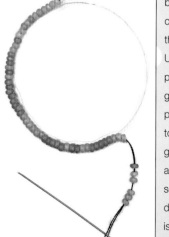

3 Lay the beaded strand carefully over the wet glaze. Use tweezers to push the beads gently into position. Try not to smudge the glaze – mistakes are fairly easy to see because it dries shiny and is not easy to remove.

backstitched fiber

rub-ons

PROUD 2 B N AMERICAN

I pledg

To Th

Of The United Sta

And To The

For Which I

One Nation Un

Indivi

With I

Jus

chipboard letters

Certain words call for emphasis. I printed words I wanted to highlight in bold and used them as a pattern for a layer of clear micro beads.

glance

America

ribbon

staples

Justice For All

1 Print type onto a sheet of white paper. (The plain paper is my test run before printing onto patterned paper.) Use two different fonts – one regular weight and a bolder font for the words that will be covered in micro beads.

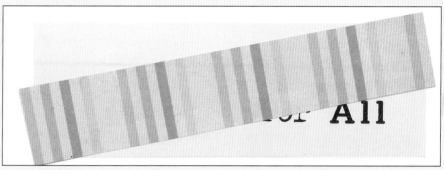

2 Align patterned paper over printed type and attach using temporary adhesive. Place this sheet back in the printer and set it to print again on the patterned paper.

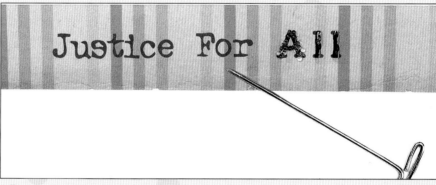

3 Trace accented words with a thin line of clear glaze and sprinkle micro beads over the wet glaze. Tap off excess beads. Use a T-pin to straighten any overlapping beads.

<table>
<tr><td colspan="2">

...for the embellishment
- white paper
- patterned paper
- computer
- clear glaze
- micro beads
- T-pin

...to make the whole page
- patterned paper
- ribbon
- chipboard letters and arrow

</td><td>

WHAT YOU NEED

- stitching rub-ons
- star stitching template
- fibers
- needle
- rubber stamps and ink pad
- rub-ons
- stapler
- adhesive (runner)

time ● ● ○
expertise ● ● ○

</td></tr>
</table>

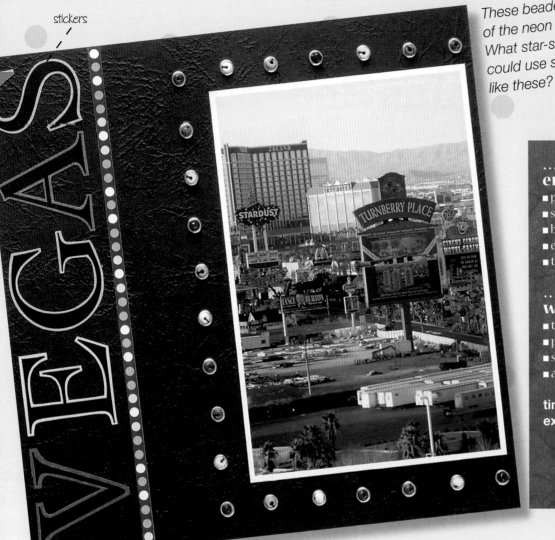

stickers

These beaded washers remind me of the neon lights of Las Vegas. What star-studded subject of yours could use some bright highlights like these?

...for the embellishment
- paper piercer or T-pin
- stitching template or ruler
- beads
- eyelet washers
- threaded needle

...to make the whole page
- textured cardstock
- patterned paper
- stickers
- adhesive (runner)

time ● ○ ○
expertise ● ○ ○

WHAT YOU NEED

✳ Tip
When poking holes, use a corkboard, foam pad, back of a mouse pad, or even a folded towel to add some cushion for the paper piercer to go through. This helps prevent damage to your work surface and dulling of the tool.

1 Use a spacing template and a paper piercer or T-pin to poke holes evenly around photo. (Or mark hole spacing with a ruler and pencil.)

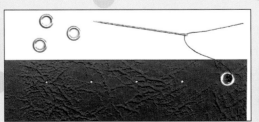

2 Anchor thread end on back of layout with a knot or adhere to layout with tape. Pull the needle and thread up through the first hole to the front of the layout and through an eyelet washer.

3 Slide a bead onto needle and thread and go down through the same hole. Gently tug thread so it remains tight and holds bead and washer securely. Push needle up through the next hole and repeat steps 2 and 3 until finished.

I wanted this title to be eye-catching and festive to capture the Thanksgiving spirit. The letters began as plain, black stickers.

THANKSgiving

Top 10 Reasons for giving Thanks

2003

tags   clips

brads —

ribbon —

buttons —

packer football

macy's thanksgiving day parade —

Little Helping Hands

Shish-ka-bob Turkey

Tryptophan Induced Naps

wishbone fights

FULL BELLIES

DADDY'S PIES

God's Blessings

Family Smiles

1 Flip a letter sticker over so that the back (adhesive side) is facing up. Thread a needle and place the longer end of the thread on adhesive letter.

2 Flip the letter over very carefully, being sure it doesn't attach itself to anything, and thread on as many beads as you need to match the width of the letter sticker.

3 Flip the sticker over so the adhesive side is facing up, and pull the thread tightly around, pressing down on adhesive. Make sure all the beads stay on the front and that the line of beads is even. Repeat with ribbon, rickrack, or another string of beads, and attach letters to layout.

...for the embellishment
- letter stickers
- ribbon
- rickrack
- seed beads
- threaded needle

- buttons
- stapler
- clips
- brads
- adhesive (runner, dots)
- computer
- sewing machine

...to make the whole page
- cardstock
- patterned paper
- metal-rimmed tags
- rub-ons
- ribbon

time ●●○
expertise ●●○

WHAT YOU NEED

Add jewelry to a scrapbook layout for a romantic personal touch. Pins like these are designed so you can customize them with your own photos. Browse the beading aisle or a thrift store for more jewelry finds for your pages.

True L

Robin and Barbara   Wedderbu

1 Kits like these come with complete instructions to help you assemble the jewelry piece. For the photo charm, first determine the size of your photo, reducing it if necessary, and trim to fit with a craft knife.

2 Position the photo under the clear self-adhesive cover. Adhere to jewelry base with adhesive. Your kit may include other components to add, like pearls and head pins.

...for the embellishment
- brooch kit
- tweezers
- small photo
- adhesive (super-hold)

WHAT YOU NEED

...to make the whole page
- cardstock
- patterned paper
- rub-ons
- adhesive (runner)

time   ● ○ ○
expertise   ● ○ ○

DON'T STOP THERE...
Add photos to small charms and attach them to a charm bracelet or to a scrapbook page. Several companies sell kits you can personalize (see Resources, p. 94).

Ðuns, Scotland '03

rub-ons

raised
stickers   die cut   rickrack   gems

how old is this

Man of Mystery

Ethan's 9th birthday '06.

The effect of this thick embossing enamel is amazing, don't you think? It's not difficult, just a little more time-consuming than regular embossing. Intrigued? See below to find the answers.

WHAT YOU NEED

...for the embellishment
- cardstock
- stamp
- seed beads
- UTEE
- clear embossing ink
- heat embossing tool

...to make the whole page
- patterned paper
- stickers
- ribbon
- gems
- die-cut arrow
- ink pad
- adhesive (runner, super-hold, foam squares)

time
expertise

1 Ink a question mark stamp with clear embossing ink. Stamp onto paper.

3 After three or four layers have been built up, with the image still hot and melted, sprinkle seed beads over image. Gently tap off loose beads and cover with more UTEE. Heat set and repeat this step to fill in any holes.

2 Sprinkle UTEE over the stamped image and set using a heat embossing tool. Repeat this step several times to get a thick layer. Working fast helps. Don't let the image cool; apply more UTEE as soon as the previous layer melts.

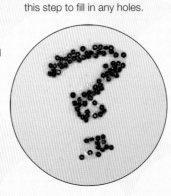

Tip
UTEE is short for Ultra Thick Embossing Enamel. It has large granules that leave a thicker impression than regular embossing powder. I used clear; it's also available in colors.

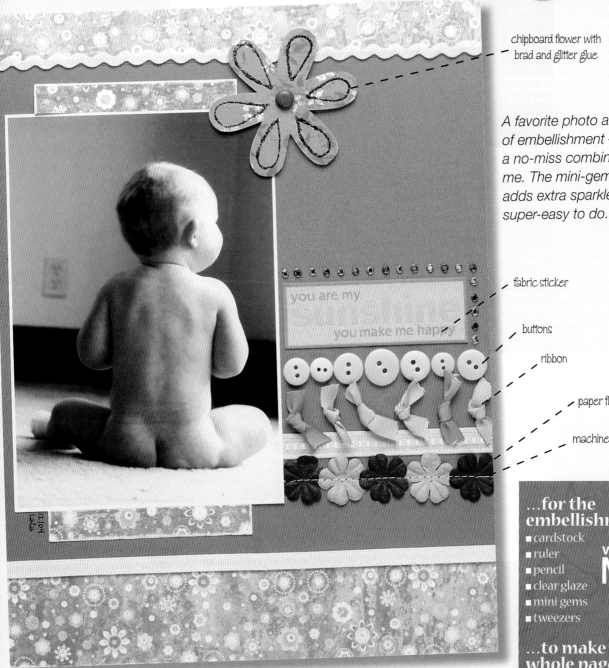

chipboard flower with
brad and glitter glue

*A favorite photo and lots
of embellishment – that's
a no-miss combination for
me. The mini-gem border
adds extra sparkle, and it's
super-easy to do.*

you are my

you make me happy

fabric sticker

buttons

ribbon

paper flowers

machine stitching

WHAT YOU NEED

...for the embellishment
- cardstock
- ruler
- pencil
- clear glaze
- mini gems
- tweezers

...to make the whole page
- fabric sticker
- patterned paper
- ribbon
- rickrack
- buttons
- paper flowers
- chipboard flower with brad
- glitter glue
- adhesive (runner, strips, dots, foam squares)
- sewing machine

time ● ○ ○
expertise ● ○ ○

1 On the cardstock, make marks to frame the fabric sticker every ¼ in. (6mm).

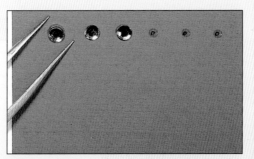

2 Carefully drop a tiny bead of clear glaze on each mark. Use tweezers to place a mini gem on each drop. Let dry.

ribbon

hand-stitched letters

2 Little Tomboys

They may prefer cute little dresses over jeans, but there are always holes in their tights. They chase lightning bugs at dusk with glass jars in hand, but always run back with slimy nightcrawlers, grasshoppers or crickets instead. And they'll choose the ballet over a movie any day, but they will still climb over the seats! Yes, these are my beautiful, girly girl tomboys! They love all the things about being girls, but they can't resist the urge to have some good old fashioned dirty fun! We'd better start saving now...not for college but for 4-wheelers! Photo taken in Jump River Wisconsin, May 2005.

The key-and-tag embellishment would work well with many other themes – new home, a teen's driving license, travel, and more. Here it works for my four-wheelin' buddies. Hand stitch the evergreens following a template or create your own shapes.

* **Tip**
Try your local hardware store for keys in many colors, shapes, and sizes. Or buy tiny journals with a lock and key at your local dollar store and use the journal for another creative project.

1 Purchase a die-cut tag or cut your own.

fibers —

2 Using an overhand knot, tie three color-coordinating fibers around the hole in the top of the tag.

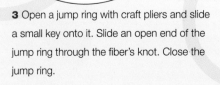

...for the embellishment
- die-cut tag
- fibers
- jump rings
- mini keys
- craft pliers

WHAT YOU NEED

...to make the whole page
- cardstock
- patterned paper
- die-cut letters
- embroidery needle and thread
- ribbon
- circle punch
- hole punch
- adhesive (runner, foam squares)
- computer
- sewing machine

time ● ● ○
expertise ● ● ○

3 Open a jump ring with craft pliers and slide a small key onto it. Slide an open end of the jump ring through the fiber's knot. Close the jump ring.

covered chipboard letters

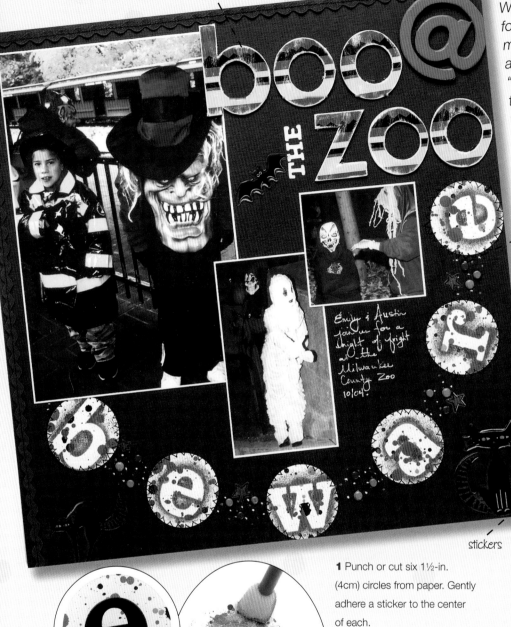

What's more appropriate for a Halloween layout than masking? That's how I created the letters that spell "beware." I also painted the "@" symbol and distressed my title letters.

mini brads

stickers

WHAT YOU NEED

...for the embellishment

- circle punch or template
- patterned paper
- letter sticker
- dauber
- acrylic paint (red, pumpkin)

...to make the whole page

- cardstock
- patterned paper
- theme stickers
- letter stickers
- "@" sign paper clip
- chipboard letters
- ribbon
- adhesive (runner, super-hold)
- white gel pen
- mini brads
- sewing machine

time ●●○
expertise ●●○

1 Punch or cut six 1½-in. (4cm) circles from paper. Gently adhere a sticker to the center of each.

2 Lightly dip the end of a dauber into the first color of acrylic paint. Blot off excess and gently dab around the sticker. Distribute the paint evenly around the sticker and be sure to cover the corners carefully. Let dry.

3 Repeat step 2 with a second color. Use the second color sparingly, allowing the first color to show through. Let dry. When paint is dry, carefully peel off the sticker to reveal your masked letter shape.

Tip ✱

Before adhering the sticker onto patterned paper, stick it to your T-shirt or pants to make it a little less tacky. You'll be able to remove it more easily without tearing the paper.

This necklace is pretty enough to wear, but I used it to frame a single photo. I rolled beautiful patterned paper into handmade beads and strung them with color-coordinated frosted glass beads.

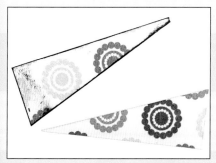

1 Cut patterned paper into small triangles, approximately 2 x 1 in. (5 x 2.5cm). Ink edges of triangles with dark ink.

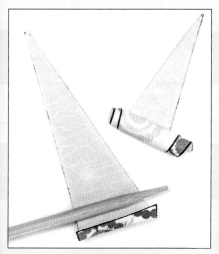

2 Roll large end of a triangle around a wood skewer, small paintbrush, or dowel. As you roll the triangle, dot edges with glaze (or other liquid glue) so the bead stays rolled.

3 Apply a coat of clear glaze over the entire bead. Let dry.

ribbon

monogram letters

...for the embellishment
- patterned paper
- dark ink pad
- wood skewer
- clear glaze

...to make the whole page
- glass beads
- embroidery needle and thread
- ribbon
- stickers
- monogram letters
- adhesive (runners, dots, strips)

WHAT YOU NEED

time ● ● ○

expertise ● ○ ○

stickers

JACK of all trades

Maybe you have a Jack or a Jill who can do everything around the house. Try this embellishment! A few snips of beaded chain go a long way to brighten up a home-improvement page.

WHAT YOU NEED

...for the embellishment
- ruler
- patterned paper
- beaded chain
- adhesive (super-hold)
- wire cutters

...to make the whole page
- patterned paper
- die-cut sayings
- stickers
- rub-ons
- adhesive (runner, foam squares)

time ● ○ ○
expertise ● ○ ○

die-cut sayings

✳ Tip

If you can't find the exact patterned paper that I used, try scanning or making a color copy of some wood and a tape measure to use on your page.

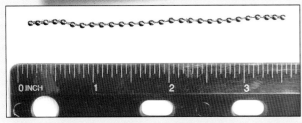

1 Measure desired length of beaded chain and cut with a wire cutters.

2 Cut a narrow strip of super-hold tape the same length as the beaded chain. Adhere to patterned paper.

3 Press beaded chain into the adhesive with firm pressure.

✳ Tip

Your local hardware store may carry beaded chain as well as other odds and ends for nifty fix-it embellishments.

I love this technique because it looks like stained glass. It also looks harder than it really is. Choose a die-cut shape with a lot of open space for the paint to show through.

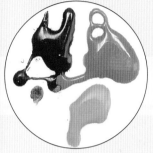

1 Pour small pools of several colors of paint onto white cardstock.

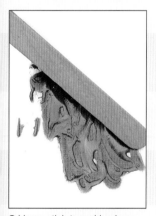

2 Use a stick to swirl colors together just slightly. Too much mixing will create a muddy color. The colors should stay bright and chunky in appearance.

rub-ons

ribbon

punched leaves

✳ Tip

Use warm colors for a fall layout (yellow, orange, red) and cool for winter (white, light gray, blue).

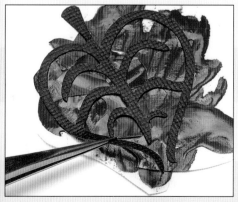

3 Gently place die cut over paint and let dry. Cut away excess paint.

...for the embellishment
- cardstock
- acrylic paint (red, pumpkin, yellow)
- wood stick or palette knife
- tweezers
- die-cut leaves

...to make the whole page
- swirl punch
- leaf punch
- ribbon
- rub-ons
- adhesive (runner, vellum runner, dots)

WHAT YOU NEED

time	● ○ ○
expertise	● ○ ○

machine stitching

wood tag

6 YEARS OLD 2006

yourself

I love that you are

content being

BLossom
sweetness
create DReam
bloom INSPIRE
BeLieVe sweetness
INSPIRE
create DReam
BLossom blooom INSPIRE
BeLieVe sweetne
imagine

create DReam
bloom

hand stitching

torn paper flowers

Snippets of knotted ribbon add bright color and varied textures to the centers of these paper flowers.

Roses are red, violets are blue, adding flowers to a layout . . . so easy to do!

...for the embellishment
- ribbon
- paper flowers
- adhesive (dots)

WHAT YOU NEED

...to make the whole page
- patterned paper
- fibers
- embroidery needle
- wood tag
- die-cut letters
- stamps and ink pad
- lettering template
- marker or pen
- adhesive (runner, dots, foam squares)
- sewing machine

time ● ● ○
expertise ● ○ ○

1 Cut five strips of ribbon in 2-in. (5cm) lengths for each flower on layout.

2 Tie a tight knot in the center of each ribbon.

> Tip

If you're looking for color inspiration, sometimes you don't have to look any further than your background paper. The colors there gave me the palette for the ribbons, flowers, tag, and other embellishments.

3 Apply an adhesive dot in the center of each flower and stick the ribbon knot to the dot. Repeat for each ribbon.

Set aside an afternoon or evening to play with some polymer clay! You can come up with some great embellishments, although it takes some planning because the clay needs to be baked. These cookies have beaded highlights that are just the right finishing touch.

 — staples

$500 REWARD.
NAKED COWGIRL

LAST SEEN:
snatching cookies from the jar
pulling the dog's tail
drawing on the walls with a dry erase marker
spilling a quart of juice on the floor
peeing on the landing
and for just plain being adorable
because that's who you are!

torn paper

...for the embellishment
- polymer clay
- acrylic roller or wood dowel
- shape cutters
- beads

...to make the whole page
- patterned paper
- ink
- chalks
- staples and stapler
- adhesive (runner, super-hold)
- computer

time ●○○
expertise ●○○

WHAT YOU NEED

Tip ✳

Mix custom colors at the same time you knead the clay to condition it. To get a range of tans and browns, try mixing small amounts of ivory or terra cotta with brown until you get shades you like.

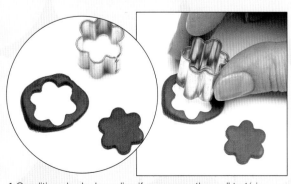

1 Condition clay by kneading if necessary, then roll to ⅛ in. (3mm) thick. Use a cutter to punch shapes or design a template and cut your own flower shapes. You can combine two or more colors of clay to mix your own colors if you like.

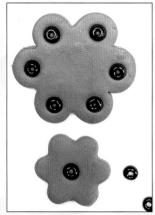

2 Gently but firmly, push beads into clay flowers.

3 For larger flower, make a light imprint of a circle in the middle of the flower with a small circle shape such as a marker cap or another clay cutter. Bake according to package directions. Cool before adhering to layout.

There's a lot to look at and read here! Break up long journaling and add color and dimension with mini brads. I printed the journaling onto a transparency first.

chipboard letter

QUIRKY little things abou

rickrack

chipboard letter outlines

stickers

tag

chipboard with ribbon binding

...for the embellishment
- patterned paper
- printable transparency
- paper piercer or T-pin
- brads
- computer

...to make the whole page
- cardstock
- patterned paper
- chipboard letters
- ribbon
- rickrack
- mini brads
- hole punch
- monogram stickers
- letter stickers
- rub-ons
- ink pad
- metal-rimmed tag
- adhesive (runner, foam squares)

WHAT YOU NEED

time	● ● ○
expertise	● ● ○

I love swimming but I don't like getting wet • My back can't be touching my pillow as I fall asleep • I'm obsessed with cleaning • I love to fly in airplanes • My favorite movie is "While You Were Sleeping" • I eat one food item at a time during a meal and I can't have any of them touching each other •

1 Computer-journal onto transparency using a bullet (dot) after each sentence. Print onto transparency.

2 Use a paper piercer (or T-pin) to poke holes through each bullet point, piercing through the transparency and patterned background paper.

love swimming but I don't like getting wet • My back can't be touching my pillow as I fall asleep • I'm obsessed with cleaning • I love to fly in airplanes • My favorite movie is "While You Were Sleeping" • I eat one food item at a time during a meal and I can't have any of them touching each other

I love swimming but I don't like getting wet • My back can't be touching my pillow as I fall asleep • I'm obsessed with cleaning • I love to fly in airplanes • My favorite movie is "While You Were Sleeping" • I eat one food item at a time during a meal and I can't have any of them touching each other

3 Attach mini brads through transparency and patterned paper.

My mom remembers when letter beads like these were used on little bracelets that identified newborns. I love the look and use letter beads for names, places, descriptive words, and more.

jewels

vellum flowers

rickr

A B E L
A S S I

After LeeAnne and Josh's wedding, we had some time to waste. Behind the church was a John Deere lot. We let the girls climb their wiggles out on the tractors. Of course it was the perfect backdrop for a photo shoot too. Adorable little girls in their Sunday best climbing around like monkeys! Sept. 2005.

JOHN DEERE

3

Little

de

L C
A U D I A

44

1 Once your layout is in place and everything is adhered securely, use a template to trace a circle very lightly with a pencil, stopping where it meets the photo.

2 Punch out many flower shapes using different colors of vellum and adhere them around the circle with vellum tape. (Plan on one flower for each letter in your word or name.)

3 Place a letter bead on each flower and adhere using small adhesive dots.

DON'T STOP THERE...
Cover a file box with letter beads and other favorite embellishments. Make it a "secret stuff" box, a recipe box, or a keepsake box. Use clear glaze to attach the letter beads securely.

AND WHILE YOU'RE AT IT...
Use leftover vellum flowers to make up a quick thank-you card.

...for the embellishment
- photo
- circle template
- pencil
- vellum (several colors)
- flower punches
- letter beads
- adhesive (vellum runner, dots)

...to make the whole page
- cardstock
- patterned paper
- ribbon
- rickrack
- stamps
- jewels
- chipboard number and letters
- flower die cuts
- acrylic paint (pumpkin, white, red, sepia)
- paintbrush
- printable transparency
- adhesive (runner, dots, vellum runner)
- computer

WHAT YOU NEED

time ● ● ●
expertise ● ○ ○

chipboard number and letters

ribbons

stamped
acrylic paint

torn edges

In this dinosaur border, the acrylic paints don't stick to the areas with embossing powder. Try different colors of powder for totally different looks.

Every other year the Dinosaur exhibit comes to the zoo. It's very exciting to see these enormous mechanical animals come to life! The zoo makes it as real as possible with stomping noises, screeching sounds and a dinosaur that spits water out its mouth. The girls love this one and wait just in front of it until they get wet! They even have one dinosaur that is only half covered so that the children can see that they are only "pretend" real and how they actually move. The exhibition is extraordinary and we never miss it! 5/06

WHAT YOU NEED

...for the embellishment
- cardstock
- dinosaur stamps
- embossing powder
- heat embossing tool
- thinned acrylic paint (various colors)
- small paintbrush
- paper towel

...to make the whole page
- cardstock
- patterned paper
- letter stamps
- ribbon
- adhesive (runner, strips)
- white gel pen
- computer

time
expertise

1 Ink stamp with clear ink. Stamp onto cardstock.

2 Sprinkle clear embossing powder over stamped image, tap off excess, and melt powder with an embossing heat tool until set (about 10 seconds).

3 Thin the acrylic colors with water. Using a soft paintbrush, cover entire stamped image with various colors. Remove excess paint with a paper towel. Let dry.

Seed beads are a subtle, three-dimensional accent for the flowers in the background paper. Thread a needle and get stitching!

1 Poke holes through flower centers using a paper piercer or T-pin. Protect the work surface with a pad.

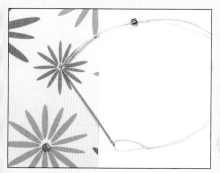

2 Thread needle and pull from back of layout to front, securing back with tape. Slide a bead onto threaded needle and insert needle back through the same hole. Come up through the next hole and repeat until done with first color.

3 Change thread color for next set of flowers/beads and repeat step 2 until all beads are sewn.

ribbon

safety-pinned charm

I adore this photo of you.

It captures your essence...

your sweetness and innocence.

I love you Isabel.

✳ Tip
Don't worry if you don't have an exact match of thread color to your beads. I use white for most light-color beads and black with dark beads.

...for the embellishment
- paper piercer or T-pin and pad
- patterned paper
- seed beads
- threaded needle
- safety pin
- ribbon
- flower charm
- adhesive (runner, strips)
- computer

WHAT YOU NEED

...to make the whole page
- cardstock
- rub-ons

time ● ○ ○
expertise ● ○ ○

shark's tooth!

metal-rimmed tags

craft netting

Underwater
Adventures
Aquarium

The beaded-ribbon borders at the top of these pages came on a card, ready to attach. The netting was a lucky find at a craft store. Both embellishments look like they took some time, but this was quite a quick-and-easy layout.

1 Start with a packaged beaded-ribbon border.

2 If your border isn't self-stick (mine wasn't), attach a line of adhesive to back of ribbon and adhere to page

Our first experience at the Mall was exploring the sea on Sunday morning! The girls had so much fun touching REAL sharks and sting rays and riding the moving sidewalk! We were encompassed by sea creatures and felt like we were swimming among them. We all learned so much.

Even though Claudia couldn't take home the "fake" treasure at the end of the tunnel, both girls did find a little sea souvenir to bring back to Wisconsin.

button

Tip

To apply ribbon onto layouts, I like to use Zips Adhesive Lines. It's easy to peel the thin, narrow strip from the backing paper and apply to ribbon evenly, and it's strong enough to hold heavy items.

DON'T STOP THERE...
Cover a small file box with colorful background papers and your favorite embellishments – including a beaded-ribbon border.

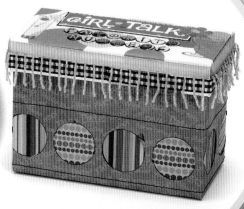

Gesso on stamp

Recognize which one is me? Our snow family portrait turned out so well, I wanted to create the perfect snowman accent to accompany it.

Family *portrait*

One beautiful and quiet winter afternoon, the entire family grabbed some mittens and replicated our family in a snow sculpture! When we finished our creation, our snow family looked so cute and cozy. This family portrait turned out so perfect, I considered using it for our holiday cards! '05

machine stitching   rub-ons

...for the embellishment
- cardstock
- foam snowman stamp
- gesso
- paintbrush
- seed beads

...to make the whole page
- cardstock
- patterned paper
- rub-ons
- adhesive (runner)
- computer
- sewing machine

WHAT YOU NEED

time ● ○ ○
expertise ● ○ ○

Tip
Gesso is thick and can slip easily on cardstock (where you don't want it!). Stamp with light pressure and remove the stamp gently for good results. Wash your stamp right away so the gesso doesn't dry on it.

2 Use a paintbrush to add more gesso to the stamped image. You want a nice thick layer so the beads sink in.

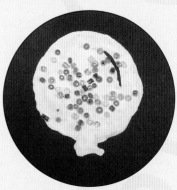

3 Sprinkle beads over the wet gesso and push down gently to ensure a good grip. Let dry.

1 Paint a chunky stamp with gesso. Press stamp onto cardstock gently.

Daisies in all shapes and sizes tie this layout together. The results of the beaded daisy chain pattern are well worth the effort!

...for the embellishment
- seed beads (two colors)
- 26-gauge craft wire
- ruler
- craft pliers
- wire cutters

WHAT YOU NEED

...to make the whole page
- cardstock
- patterned paper
- vellum
- Delight modeling compound
- chalk
- ribbon
- plastic buckle
- adhesive (runner, dots)
- computer

time ●●●
expertise ●●○

ribbon with buckle

Laurelei

You were 3 months old when you were baptized and I was worried you'd be too big to fit into Gram's handmade Christening gown. Our church had been searching for a new minister for years and finally found Pastor Julie. Needless to say, you were her first Christening and everything went beautifully. Not only did you just fit into the traditional gown, you were the happiest baby! July 11, 2004

daisy made with modeling compound and colored with chalk.

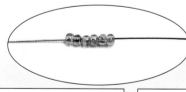

1a Cut 1 yd. (.9m) of 26-gauge craft wire. Turn a loop at one end to keep beads from sliding off.
b String six Color A beads onto the wire and push them to the loop end.

2 Slide the free end of the wire through the bead closest to the loop.

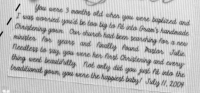

3 Add a Color B bead to the wire.

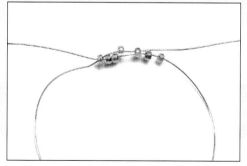

4 Thread the wire through the fourth Color A bead.

5 Pull to tighten so beads form a flower shape. Repeat steps 1b through 5, adding a Color B bead between each flower until the chain measures 12 in. (30cm). Use adhesive dots (or wire fasteners) to attach the chain to page.

Sure, you usually expect to see ants at a picnic. I used ladybugs instead, just because of their cute factor!

Riverside PICNIC

SICLES
COOKIES
ATE
SANDWICH
GRILLED CH
FRUIT SALA
CORN ICE
BRATWURST K
CHIP COOKIES
GRILLED CHIC
POTATO SA
BEANS PU
CORN ON T
SALAD
CHIP COO
HOT DOGS PAST
PICKLE RELISH
OLIVES JUI
CORN ON THE COB
FRUIT SALAD
POPSICLES
COOKIES
TOMATOES

PICKLE RE

JOHN HAWKS PUB ON WATER STREET IN DOWNTOWN MILWAUKEE IS ONE OF MY FAVORITE PLACES TO EAT. THE CHEESE CURDS ARE SO DELICIOUS AND THE CORNED BEEF SANDWICHES ARE FANTASTIC. IT MAKES MY MOUTH WATER JUST WRITING ABOUT THEM. AND THE KOSHER DILL PICKLES. I COULD GO ON AND ON! YUM! THIS MOTHER'S DAY WAS SO WARM AND SCENIC. SITTING THERE ALONG THE MILWAUKEE RIVER. NO CHILDREN. JUST MY MOM, BRO AND GRANDMA. RELAXING AND CHATTING.   MAY 2005

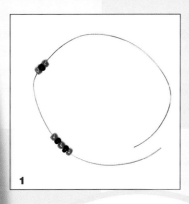

1

2

1 Cut 10 in. (25cm) of 26-gauge craft wire. String eight beads onto wire in this pattern: red, black, red, black, red, red, black, red. These will be the first and second rows of the ladybug. Separate the beads into two groups. The first group of five beads will be the red, black, red, black, red beads and the other group of three should contain the red, black, red.

2 Pass the right end of the wire through the group of five beads (but not through the group of three). Pull tight so the two groups of beads meet.

3

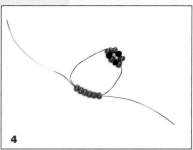

4

3 String six red beads onto the left side of the wire.

4 Pass the right end of the wire through the group of six red beads. Pull tight so the two groups meet.

5

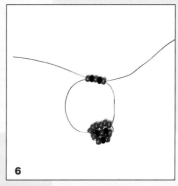

6

5 String five more beads onto the right end of wire in this order: red, black, red, black, red.

6 Pass the left end of wire through the row of five beads. Pull tight.

7

8

9

7 String three black beads onto the left end of wire.

8 Pass the right end of the wire through the group of three black beads. Pull tight.

9 Snip wire ends about ½ in. (1.3cm) above the black beads. Use a small roundnose or needlenose craft pliers to curl just the ends of the wire to form antennae.

DON'T STOP THERE...

Since all the supplies are handy, make an extra ladybug to decorate a simple "good luck" card.

good luck

...for the embellishment
- seed beads (red, black)
- 26-gauge craft wire
- ruler
- craft pliers
- wire cutters

WHAT YOU NEED

...to make the whole page
- cardstock
- patterned paper
- ink pad
- stitching rub-ons
- die cuts
- clear glaze
- adhesive (runner, strips)
- computer

time ● ● ●
expertise ● ● ○

ribbon

The trick to this technique is using clear shapes cut from a transparency sheet. You can use a report cover or even vellum. Because the base is transparent, only the glitter will show.

SALZBURG

This funny and extraordinary sculpture stood captivating my attention during a beautiful snow storm. Its long and slender lines were smooth and cold. Even though it was made of steel and balanced powerfully against its cycle, the bitter cold and ice made it appear fragile.

As I studied this amazing work of art, peeking through my scarf and hat, I giggled and took a photo of it. I wanted to bring this moment home with me. I don't want to be one of those people that live on the world and not in it. I love this sculpture and it will always remind me of my trip to Austria with my grandma and mom.   photo '98

1 Make snowflakes from transparency film using a punch or die-cutting machine.

2 Place snowflakes in a box and spray them with adhesive.

3 Sprinkle iridescent flakes over snowflakes. Press flakes into adhesive for a secure attachment and rub off excess. Add adhesive to back and adhere to layout.

...for the embellishment
- spray adhesive
- snowflake punch or die cut
- transparency film
- shallow cardboard box
- iridescent flakes

...to make the whole page
- cardstock
- patterned paper
- ribbon
- adhesive (runner)
- computer

WHAT YOU NEED

time   ● ○ ○
expertise   ● ○ ○

54

What's the next-best thing to using real sand? I devised this look-alike technique using micro beads on a vellum photo frame.

die cuts

Notice how I repeated some of the die-cut shapes and colors in the negative space of the title letters?

...for the embellishment
- acrylic paint
- paintbrush
- vellum
- clear glaze
- micro beads

WHAT YOU NEED

...to make the whole page
- cardstock
- patterned paper
- die-cut flowers
- chipboard letters
- stickers
- acrylic paint (white)
- adhesive (runner, super-hold)

time ● ● ○
expertise ● ○ ○

For Brook Park

Laurelei 2, Claudia 5, Isabel 7   7/06

beach babes

chipboard letters

stickers

1 Paint edges of vellum frame with acrylic paint. Let dry.

2 Spread clear glaze on the corners and bottom of frame.

3 Sprinkle micro beads over wet glaze and tap off excess. Allow to dry. If vellum curls, lay a sheet of waxed paper over frame and place under a heavy book until it's dry.

Tip ✳
I wanted the chipboard letters to match the background paper, so I covered them with the same print and carefully trimmed around the letters with a craft knife.

DON'T STOP THERE...
This is a wood box I covered. The frame around St. Nick's picture uses the same micro bead technique.

My mom is proud of her charms. I had fun creating a page that tells a story about her bracelet.

letter stickers

ribbon

charming

CHIT-C

It's fun trying to listen to my mom when she's ta... on. It jingles so loudly that you can hardly hear her many charms and if you ask my mom, she'll not only t... one but also what each one represents.

For example her love of travel is displayed with ... palette of colors represents her love for art. The ... characters in her life...her granddaughters of course! ... you about her bracelet...have her take it off! Other... above the bracelet's joyful sound of clanging and cli...

machine stitching

die-cut
flower with
brads

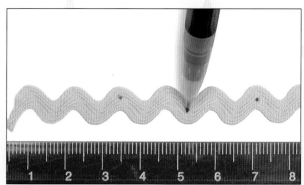

1 Cut ribbon or rickrack to desired length. Measure three marks where the jump rings will go. Note the charm size so they are not too close together.

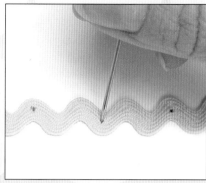

2 Poke a hole with a paper piercer or T-pin at each mark.

3 Pull a jump ring through the hole in the ribbon. Add a charm, making sure it faces you, and close the jump ring with pliers.

...for the embellishment
- rickrack or ribbon
- ruler
- pencil
- paper piercer or T-pin
- charms
- jump rings
- craft pliers

- letter stickers
- die-cut flower
- brads
- adhesive (runner, strips)
- computer
- sewing machine

time ● ● ○
expertise ● ○ ○

...to make the whole page
- cardstock
- patterned paper

WHAT YOU NEED

DON'T STOP THERE...
I made this photo frame from a card designed for giving a gift of money (banks often sell these at Christmas time). I covered the change slots with background paper, and instead of attaching the charms to ribbon, I hooked the jump rings right into the cardstock of the frame.

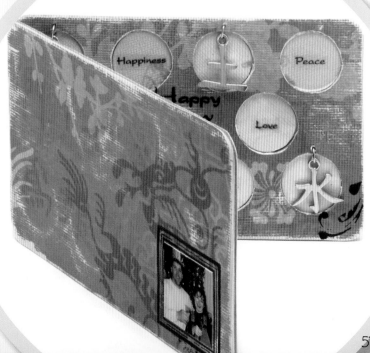

harm bracelet
acelet beholds
obtained each

charm and the
s are significant
sk her to tell
ar her chit chat
006

Labels on the layout: chipboard letters · wood tag · HOUSE · stapled ribbon

Journaling blocks on the page:

Gram's mailbox is a drive-up box. We don't have that kind at home, so the girls love to run out to the curb to retrieve Gram's mail!

Matrioshka dolls decorate Gram's living-room shelves except for when the girls are visiting. Then they are usually seen marching around the house!

The giraffe is Gram's favorite animal. She has all sorts of them around her house, but the girl's favorite two are the plush toys, Geoffrey and Geraldine.

An absolute favorite luxury the girls must indulge in when visiting overnight, is bathing in Gram's red seashell bath-tub. It comes deluxe with bath toys, bubbles and a heat lamp! Even though the bathroom is decorated in modern African style, the tub stays hidden behind a big African curtain!

Since we run lots of errands while visiting Gram, car treats are a necessity. Gram keeps them in a little treasure chest where the girls have fun picking their favorites.

What's so great about Gram's house? Lots of things! This page celebrates five of them. Beaded numbers really catch the eye.

1 Trace a number or letter onto cardstock using a lettering template. (A computer-printed letter or number will work too.)

2 Carefully trace over the letter with clear glaze.

3 Sprinkle beads over wet number or letter. Gently tap off excess beads and let dry.

die cuts with brads

It's a doggy duel, all in good fun! I mimicked the tug-o'-war with a raffia ribbon tied in knots. It works with twine or ribbon too.

...for the embellishment
- raffia or ribbon
- ruler
- beads
- jump rings
- craft pliers

WHAT YOU NEED

...to make the whole page
- cardstock
- patterned paper
- letter stickers
- die cuts
- paper piercer or T-pin
- brads
- lettering template
- white gel pen
- adhesive (runner, super-hold)

time ● ○ ○
expertise ● ○ ○

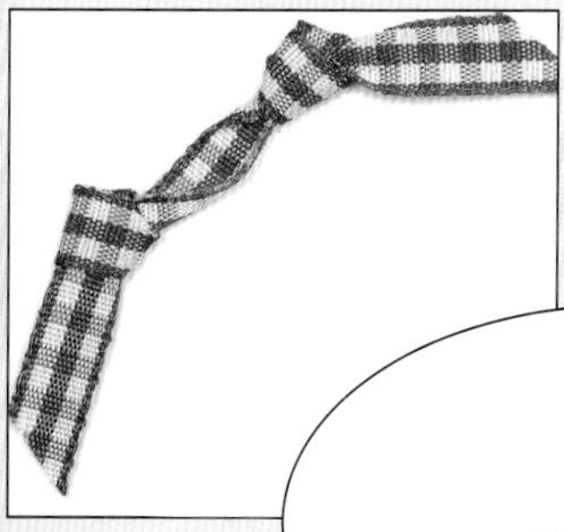

canine

Tug-o'-War

1 Cut a length of ribbon or raffia 4 in. (10cm) longer than the finished length. Tie as many knots as desired, but don't pull the knots too tight.

2 Using a craft pliers, open a jump ring enough to slide a bead onto it, then slide the jump ring through a knot in the ribbon.

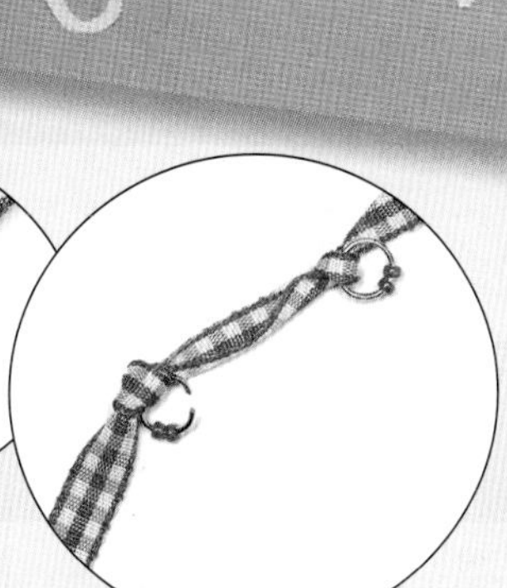

3 Close the jump ring with pliers and tuck the closure under the knot of the ribbon. Pull the knot tight. Repeat for each knot.

rub-ons

chipboard letters

'my little

gold[i]

Lo[o]

has big

Attitude-

and I love it!

vellum word

PATTERN
page
92

I created the butterfly outline with flowers punched from a variety of paper and thin cork. Hand stitching finishes it off. I sprinkled flowers across the title for a nice touch of repetition.

punched
flowers

jewels

1 Use at least two different flower punches to cut many small flowers from a variety of coordinating cardstock, textured paper, and cork. I punched approximately 55 for the butterfly shape.

2 Cut butterfly (or other) shape from vellum and adhere flowers around edge, alternating the flower shapes and colors.

...for the embellishment

- flower punches
- thin cork sheet
- cardstock
- textured paper
- vellum
- mini brads
- assorted jewels and sequins
- adhesive (dots)

...to make the whole page

- patterned paper
- chipboard letters
- stitching rub-ons
- die-cut letters
- letter stickers
- paper piercer or T-pin
- fiber
- embroidery needle
- additional assembled flowers
- acrylic paint (white, pink, red)
- vellum word
- clear glaze
- adhesive (runner, vellum runner, super-hold)

WHAT YOU NEED

time ● ● ●
expertise ● ● ○

3 Decorate each flower with a jewel, brad, or sequin.

Stencil filled with micro beads

die-cut sayings

Bob

LOVE

100% Unconditional Love

Precious

Sweet & Simple

simply perfect

machine stitching

rub-ons

I made my own stencil, then filled it with sparkling micro beads for a subtle, beautiful focal point. Die cuts and stitching top off the embellishment.

WHAT YOU NEED

...for the embellishment
- letter stencils
- pencil
- cardstock
- craft knife
- clear glaze
- micro beads

...to make the whole page
- cardstock
- patterned paper
- die-cut sayings
- rub-ons
- emery board
- adhesive (runner)
- sewing machine

time ● ○ ○
expertise ● ○ ○

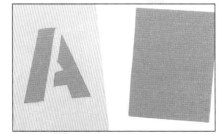

1 For the letter frame, trace stencil letter onto cardstock with a pencil.

2 Use a craft knife to cut out the letter. Erase any leftover pencil marks. Cut another piece of paper a bit larger than the letter but smaller than the frame. Adhere behind the letter.

3 Distribute a thin coat of clear glaze evenly inside the stencil letter. (Too much will create a cluster of lumpy beads.) Sprinkle beads onto wet surface and shake off excess. Let dry.

62

I hand stitched to accent the fish shapes. French knots are a good stand-in for bubbles.

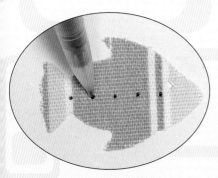

1 Cut a fish shape using a die-cutting machine or large punch. Adhere to layout. Using a spacing ruler (or a ruler and pencil), poke five holes ¼ in. (.6cm) apart across the middle of each fish. Punch three more holes vertically coming from the mouth of the fish.

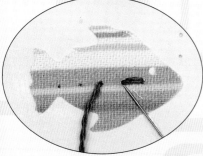

2 Thread a needle with fibers or embroidery floss and backstitch across the center of the fish. Tape ends down on back of cardstock.

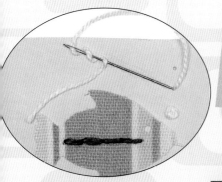

3 To create bubbles, make a French knot in each of the three holes coming from the mouth of the fish.

Need help with backstitch or French knots?
You'll find stitching directions on p. 93.

Male Bonding

male (mal) bond·ing (bon'ding) n. An emotional masculine connection occurring between another of its gender. Finding companionship with another during football games, fishing in the rain, grilling meat and hunting for anything.

ribbon

paper clip

...for the embellishment
- fish die cut
- striped fabric or paper
- ruler
- pencil
- paper piercer or T-pin
- embroidery needle and thread
- fiber

...to make the whole page
- patterned paper
- ribbon
- stamps and ink pad
- paper clip
- adhesive (runner, strips)
- computer

WHAT YOU NEED

time ●○○
expertise ●●○

chipboard letter

ribbon

b is for **Blustery Day!**

Claudia was so cute trying to walk in the blusty rain this autumn day. The wind was tough but she held on to that umbrella! It almost picked her up and whisked her away! I told her I'd hate if the wind blew my sweet little girl away and she answered "The wind isn't blowing this sweet little girl anywhere!"

Claudia 3 yrs 10/04

metal-rimmed tag

Chunky stamps work great with acrylic paint – and the bolder the image, the better. Use a fine-tip paintbrush to add details after the stamped image dries – dots, outlines, and curves.

Tip

A used CD makes a great paint palette. When one side is dry, use the other side, then just throw it away.

...for the embellishment
- foam stamps (leaves, swirls)
- foam paintbrush
- fine-tip paintbrush
- acrylic paint (red, white, red-orange, yellow, burnt umber, black, plum)

...to make the whole page
- cardstock
- patterned paper
- metal-rimmed tag
- ribbon
- chipboard letter
- rub-ons
- lettering template
- white gel pen
- adhesive (runner, vellum runner, peel-and-stick sheet)
- computer

WHAT YOU NEED

time	● ● ○	
expertise	● ○ ○	

1 Using acrylic paints and a small foam paintbrush, brush paint onto a chunky foam or rubber stamp.

2 Position painted stamp on layout and press gently for even coverage. Lift carefully and allow to dry. Wash stamp immediately.

3 Decorate the stamped image with a fine paintbrush. (You also can use the paint bottle if it comes with a small applicator tip.)

I love making these letter beads, and they have lots of uses. I used them here as part of the page title. You can use this technique to make some playful jewelry too!

letter stickers

brads

machine stitching

...for the embellishment

- Delight modeling compound
- clay cutter
- letter stamps
- dye-based ink (black, yellow)
- T-pin
- fiber
- embroidery needle
- pearl beads

WHAT YOU NEED

...to make the whole page

- patterned paper
- stickers
- mini brads
- self-adhesive ink-jet transparency
- adhesive (runner)
- computer
- sewing machine

time ● ● ○
expertise ● ● ○

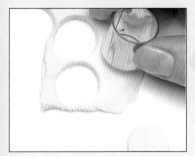

1 Roll modeling compound to ¼ in. (6mm) thickness. Use a 1¼ in. (3cm) circle clay cutter to cut a circular base for each letter from modeling compound.

2 With a T-pin, gently and carefully make a hole through the bead from side to side. (To help guide the pin through the modeling compound, place your thumb on the bottom of the circle and index finger on the top.) Using a dye-based ink, stamp a letter on the circle. Air dry.

3 Use a different color ink to highlight the edge of the letter bead. Thread a needle, knot the thread, add a pearl bead, tie another knot, and add a second pearl bead. Next, spell the word in beads, adding a pearl bead between each letter bead. Add a pearl bead to the end and tie a knot.

Because I'm right-handed, I found it easiest to spell the words working from right to left.

I designed this embellishment to reflect all the beauty and energy of July 4th sparklers and fireworks. Make your own with sparkling beads and star sequins.

FREEDOM

this year

every year

celebrate

America

machine
stitching

photos 2005 - Isabel 2006

PATTERN
page
92

See backstitch instructions on p. 93.

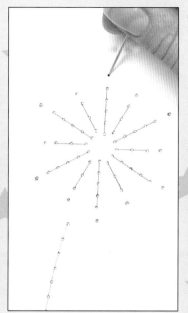

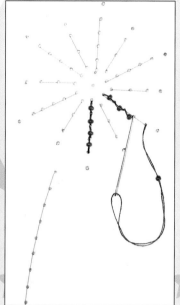

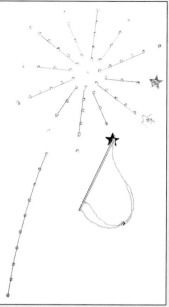

1 Using the pattern on p. 92 (or your own design), poke holes with a paper piercer or T-pin through the template onto your layout. (To protect your work surface, use a pad underneath.) Lightly connect the dots with a pencil to help guide your stitching.

2 Bring the needle from the back of the paper through the hole. Knot or tape thread on the back to secure. Slide a bead onto the needle and thread. Insert the needle into the next hole and pull tight underneath. Follow the backstitch sequence for each stitch.

3 For stars, bring the needle up through the back of the hole and slide a star and a bead onto the needle and thread. Insert the needle back through the star and into the same hole. Repeat for each star.

...for the embellishment

- patterned paper or card-stock
- paper piercer or T-pin and pad
- pencil
- threaded needle
- silver stars
- seed beads

WHAT YOU NEED

...to make the whole page

- patterned paper
- letter stickers
- lettering template
- black marker or pen
- adhesive (runner)
- sewing machine

time ● ● ○
expertise ● ○ ○

DON'T STOP THERE...
Use the embellishment technique you just learned to create this cute framed flower art from punched circles.

This embellishment takes a little time and patience. I like the dimension it adds.

buttons

giant rickrack

machine stitching

ribbon

backstitched fiber

...for the embellishment
- covered button kit
- fabric
- fibers
- embroidery needle
- pencil
- wire cutters

...to make the whole page
- patterned paper
- fibers
- ribbon
- giant rickrack
- monogram letters
- letter stickers
- rub-ons
- buttons
- adhesive (runner, strips, foam squares, dots)
- computer
- sewing machine

time ● ● ●
expertise ● ● ◐

WHAT YOU NEED

1 Cut a circle from fabric that is about ¾ in. (2cm) larger all around than the button cover.

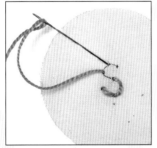

2 Lightly draw a letter on the center of the fabric (freehand or using a lettering template). Backstitch the letter shape.

3 Use wire cutters to snip off the loop on the button back.

4 Tack the back of the fabric letter to the button cover with adhesive. Flip button over and tuck the excess fabric under the button cover. Push button into the back of the button cover, keeping all fabric tucked tightly.

Song lyrics © 2000 Stuart Stotts. Used with permission.

Using glue, you can place a lot of beads in a short time. The combination of glued and stitched beads creates swirls of movement on my boating page. I added a few inked curves as well.

WHAT YOU NEED

...for the embellishment
- French curve (or pattern, p. 93)
- pencil
- clear glaze
- tweezers
- seed beads

...to make the whole page
- cardstock
- patterned paper
- embroidery needle
- fibers
- rub-on letters
- stickers
- ribbon
- white gel pen
- adhesive (runner, vellum runner)

time ● ● ○
expertise ● ● ○

PATTERN page **93**

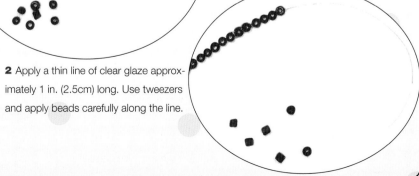

Faster! Faster!

Lake Lucerne

Karen
Evan
Alex
August '02

1 With a pencil, lightly trace around a French curve (or use the pattern on p. 93).

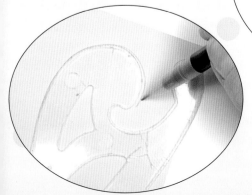

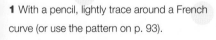

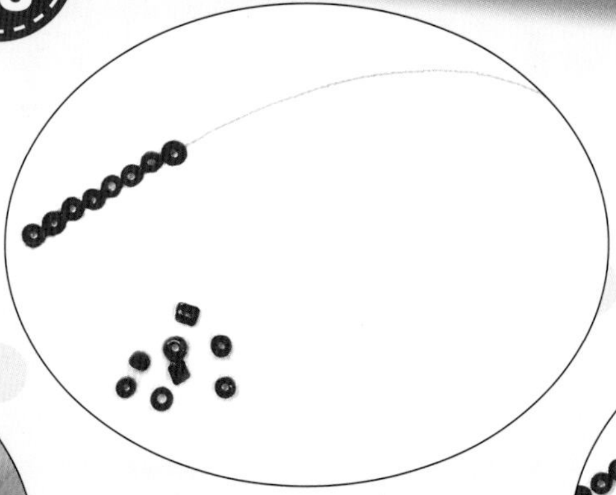

2 Apply a thin line of clear glaze approximately 1 in. (2.5cm) long. Use tweezers and apply beads carefully along the line.

3 Repeat step 2 until the entire curve is covered in beads. For the stitched beaded curve, follow the technique used on the "Freedom" layout (p. 66).

die-cut letters

PATTERN
page
92

SwEet & sOuR

BRIAN

...for the embellishment
- cardstock scrap
- embroidery needle
- embroidery floss in two colors
- beads

...to make the whole page
- patterned paper
- colored vellum
- ribbon
- chipboard sayings
- die-cut letters
- letter rub-ons
- stickers
- beads
- craft wire
- craft pliers
- ink pad
- adhesive (runner, vellum runner, dots)

WHAT YOU NEED

time ● ○ ○
expertise ● ○ ○

chipboard sayings

ribbon

The takeout box is very easy to make out of a square of colored vellum (see folding instructions, p. 92). I added a colorful tassel suspended from craft wire.

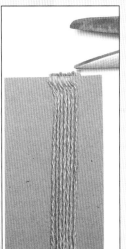

1 To create a tassel, wrap embroidery floss around a 4-in. (10cm) piece of cardstock. Wrap about eight times for a thin tassel, more for a thicker tassel. Cut threads at both ends of card and keep thread in a bundle with ends together.

2 Cut a 3-in. (8cm) piece of embroidery floss and fold in half.

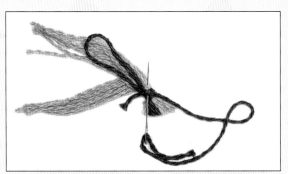

4 Fold the threads around the binding and secure by binding another piece of embroidery thread (as in step 3) around tassel about ¼ in. from top. Make sure the folded loop thread is sticking out from the top. String beads on loop if desired. Trim tassel ends.

3 Align ends with one group of bundle ends. Bind bundle about ¼ in. (6mm) from end by wrapping another piece of embroidery floss around bundle. Tie or sew tightly together.

1 Apply very tiny drops of clear glaze (about 8-10 drops at a time) onto the patterned paper in a design that follows or complements the pattern.

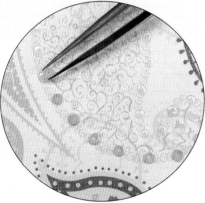

2 Using tweezers, carefully place a bead onto each drop. Let dry.

chipboard letters

machine stitching

rub-ons

Our family

Good Times together

10 feet long

forever

Sometimes I like to enhance a background pattern. I made a few paisleys pop by adding lines of seed beads.

...for the embellishment
- patterned paper
- clear glaze
- tweezers
- seed beads

...to make the whole page
- cardstock
- patterned paper
- chipboard letters
- rub-ons
- adhesive (runner)
- sewing machine

WHAT YOU NEED

time ●●○
expertise ●○○

Cranberry Fest
Rules &
Regulations

the Elusive H

Names, places, important dates… just a few of the many things to record on these little metal-rimmed tags that add movement to your page.

- No Kids
- No Husbands
- No Stress
- Fried Mushrooms disguised as cheese curds ok
- must like liquidating stores
- must never drive the same route twice
- must not stare directly at shiny objects on the rd.
- must love shopping in 8" of snow, flooded fairgrounds or blazing sun (shoe shopping permitted when such conditions arise)

- must enjoy small town theatres, "Eat" restaurants, wine and cheese

Signe
Julie

Kelly

Heidi
Karen

flower charm

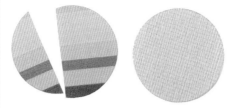

1 Cut or punch circles that fit the tag from two coordinating papers. Cut about ⅓ from one of the prints and keep the second to use as a base.

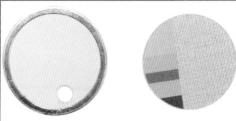

2 Adhere small piece on top of the base, then adhere to tag. This covers the original hanging hole, so punch a new one with a hole punch.

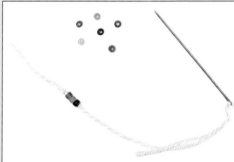

3 Using one strand of embroidery thread, thread needle, knot end, and add six or seven seed beads. Loop through hole in tag and attach to layout.

DON'T STOP THERE...
Make a Christmas count-down tree using a similar technique. These tags were hung from earring wires so they could be moved around easily.

Micro beads over die cut

letters printed on transparency

WHERE IN THE WORLD IS

CAMPING frog?

chipboard letters

My photo subject was Camping Frog, a multicolor, globe-trotting kind of guy. I found a frog die cut and just needed to add beads for color! With this technique, you simply cut away the adhesive backing bit by bit in order to place beads with a lot of control.

If you don't have access to a die-cutting machine, trace a pre-die-cut shape and trim with a craft knife.

1 Measure die cut and cut a piece of white cardstock and adhesive sheet a little larger than die cut. Peel backing off one side of adhesive and attach to cardstock. Trim cardstock using a die-cutting machine or by hand.

2 Use a craft knife to cut small segments of adhesive backing from the shape. Peel off the backing and sprinkle one color of beads over exposed area. Press the beads down firmly. (A brayer is helpful for making sure the beads adhere well.)

3 Repeat step 2 with other colors of beads, doing one color at a time until entire shape is filled.

I like to use long, loose stitches that look like they're attaching different background papers together. You really can't do this the wrong way; loosen up and create your own lazy, crazy stitch pattern.

rub-ons

WHAT YOU NEED

...for the embellishment
- patterned cardstock
- paper piercer or T-pin
- embroidery needle and thread

...to make the whole page
- cardstock
- patterned paper
- rub-ons
- letter stamps
- acrylic paint (wine, burnt umber, white)
- white plastic letters
- ribbon
- fibers
- self-adhesive ink-jet transparency
- adhesive (runner, strips)
- computer

time ●●○
expertise ●○○

beautifully **nappy**

ha ha ha

bed head

Laurelei has outrageous hair in the morning! She is more blonde than her sisters and when she sits at the table eating cereal, she has this halo of snarls around her head. I do prefer her beautiful curls to the snarls, but she is so cute and huggable in the morning with those sleepy eyes and nappy hair, I just can't resist hugging her so tight!   Lala - 2   4/06

love

plastic letters

ribbon

1 Using a paper piercer or T-pin, poke holes in a random pattern, about ⅛ in. (3mm) apart and about ½-1 in. (1.3-2.5cm) across from each other. It should look a little like an unbalanced starburst.

2 Using embroidery thread and needle, start sewing from the back of the layout. Knot or tape the thread end. Pull the needle to the front of the layout and back down the hole across from it.

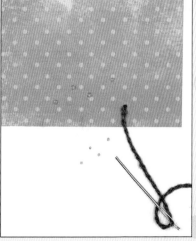

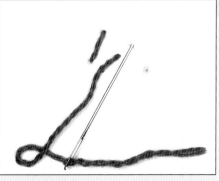

3 On the back of the layout, move the needle over to the hole next to the one you just came through. Repeat steps 2 and 3.

Bristol Renaissance Fair '06

Sir Joseph & Sebastian

I played on the Renaissance theme by giving the photo a painted, "aged" frame with burnt umber acrylic paint. To tie the page together, I repeated the brush strokes around the edges of the page. This is one of the quickest, easiest ways I know to add color and a bit of texture to a page!

1 Secure the seal between photo and layout by placing adhesive around all four sides of the back of photo. (This helps keep the photo from rippling and paint from getting under the photo.) Press photo onto layout.

2 Start by applying small amounts of paint around the corners of the photo. Gradually add more paint for a thicker and deeper color. Paint carefully around all edges of photo. Let dry.

...for the embellishment
- photo
- foam paintbrush
- acrylic paint (burnt umber)
- adhesive (super-hold)

...to make the whole page
- cardstock
- patterned paper
- rubber stamps and ink pad
- gel pens (white, black)

WHAT YOU NEED

time ● ○ ○
expertise ● ○ ○

I'll share the exact stitch instructions so you can just relax and follow them to create your own wood-bead border! It's a fantastic look for a rustic page like this Old-World adventure.

...for the embellishment
- cardstock
- ruler or spacing template
- paper piercer or T-pin
- embroidery needle and thread
- wood beads

...to make the whole page
- patterned paper
- stickers
- beads
- fibers
- adhesive (runner)
- computer
- sewing machine

WHAT YOU NEED

time ●●○
expertise ●○○

1 Using a paper piercer or T-pin, poke a row of holes about ¼ in. (6mm) apart in the cardstock. Make a second row. For the distance between the top and bottom row, measure your bead and add about ½ in. (1.3cm).

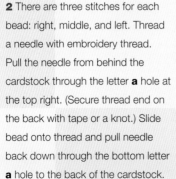

2 There are three stitches for each bead: right, middle, and left. Thread a needle with embroidery thread. Pull the needle from behind the cardstock through the letter **a** hole at the top right. (Secure thread end on the back with tape or a knot.) Slide bead onto thread and pull needle back down through the bottom letter **a** hole to the back of the cardstock. Leave just a bit of slack.

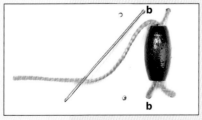

3 On the back, push the needle through the bottom letter **b** hole (middle hole) onto the front. Pull the needle through the bead and sew through the top letter **b** hole to the back side of the cardstock.

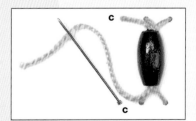

4 Once again on the back side, pull the needle through the top letter **c** hole (the left hole) onto the front. Pull the needle through the bead for the last time and down through the bottom letter **c** hole. Repeat steps 2 through 4 with additional beads until the row is finished.

Shrink-plastic beads

A recovery from lymphoma deserves a big celebration, so we went all-out on the "Survivor" theme. I used shrink plastic to make the leaves that hang from hemp – lots of fun to make.

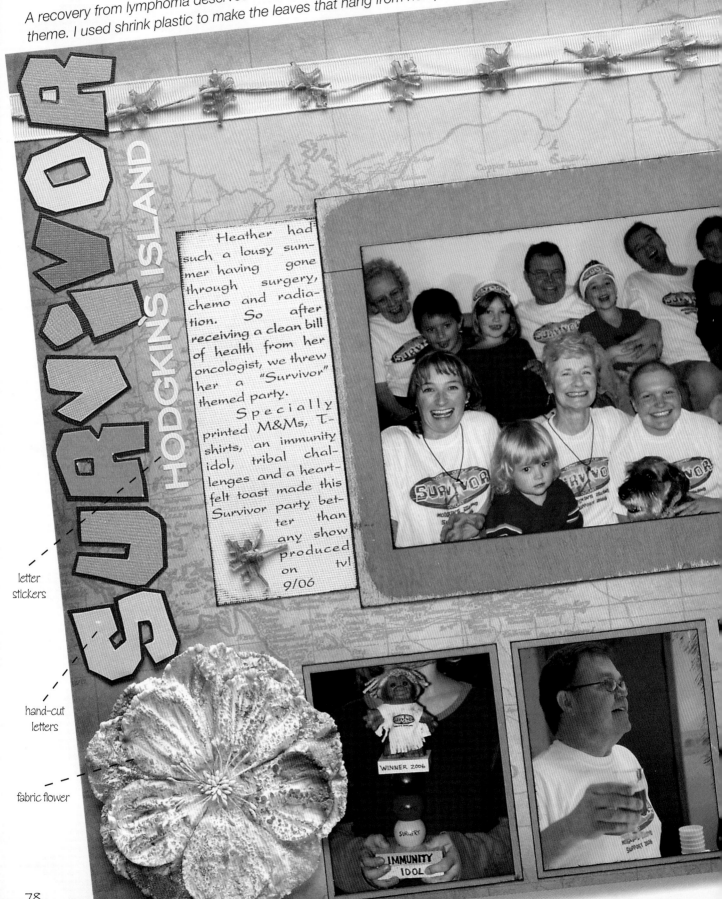

SURVIVOR

HODGKIN'S ISLAND

Heather had such a lousy summer having gone through surgery, chemo and radiation. So after receiving a clean bill of health from her oncologist, we threw her a "Survivor" themed party.

Specially printed M&Ms, T-shirts, an immunity idol, tribal challenges and a heart-felt toast made this Survivor party better than any show produced on tv! 9/06

letter stickers

hand-cut letters

fabric flower

WINNER 2006

SURGERY

IMMUNITY IDOL

1 Some shrink plastic is rough and some is smooth. If using the smooth shrink film, rough it up a little with sandpaper. To cut leaf shapes, use a jumbo punch, a die-cutting machine, or a craft knife. My leaves were about 2¼ in. (6cm) long before shrinking.

2 Lightly color the roughened surface with colored pencils. When the film shrinks, the color deepens, so apply light pressure when coloring.

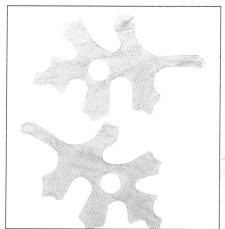

3 Using a ¼-in. (6mm) circle punch, make a hole in the center of each leaf. The ¼-in. hole may seem big, but it will be quite small once the shrink plastic is heated. Bake plastic according to package directions. Once cool, attach to layout with hemp cord or embroidery floss.

Shrink plastic reduces to about 25–30% of its original size.

...for the embellishment
- shrink plastic
- jumbo leaf punch or die cut
- colored pencils
- hole punch

...to make the whole page
- textured cardstock
- patterned paper
- stickers
- ribbon
- flower
- hemp cord
- black ink pad
- adhesive (runner, dots)
- computer

WHAT YOU NEED

time ● ● ○
expertise ● ○ ○

DON'T STOP THERE...
For the "Survivor" party favor, we ordered custom-printed M&M candies with sayings like "Outwit, Outlast" and "Hodgkin's Survivor." Make your own boxes using patterned cardstock and the pattern on p. 93. Add a shrink-plastic leaf tied with hemp.

PATTERN
page
93

A wardrobe of colorful hats inspired this page, embellished with buttons, beads, and lettering in a bright color palette that plays off the background paper.

rub-ons

is the best medicine

laughter

ha - ha - ha

buttons

1 Using a craft knife or pin, break off several staples from a strip of staples. Slightly bend one of the arms out at a 45° angle so you'll be able to load beads onto it.

2 Slide seed beads on the bent arm of staple and onto the top portion. Use only enough beads to go across the top of the staple. On a letter, mark where the two ends of the staple will go and use a pin to poke holes through the marks.

3 Push the two ends of the staple through the holes in the letter and flip the letter over. Using a pencil eraser, press the two ends of the staple flat.

...for the embellishment
- hand-cut or die-cut letters
- staples
- T-pin
- seed beads
- pencil with eraser

- self-adhesive ink-jet transparency
- rub-ons
- fiber
- brads
- adhesive (runner, dots)
- computer

...to make the whole page
- cardstock
- patterned paper
- buttons

time ● ○ ○
expertise ● ○ ○

WHAT YOU NEED

Letters can become embellishments! I made the negative space of the letter "o" into a heart, then added beads for emphasis.

chipboard letters

ribbon

...for the embellishment
- cardstock
- patterned paper
- clear glaze
- beads
- craft knife
- tweezers

WHAT YOU NEED

...to make the whole page
- patterned paper
- stickers
- vellum quote
- stapler
- buttons
- ribbon
- chipboard letters
- adhesive (runner, strips, dots)

time ●○○
expertise ●○○

Give love like your pet does. Unconditionally and without questions.

4/06

staples

vellum quote

buttons

1 Cut a circle from heavy cardstock, about the same size as the chipboard letters used for the layout. Use a craft knife to cut a heart shape from the circle.

2 Cover the "O" outline with clear glaze and sprinkle beads over the wet adhesive. Using tweezers, pack beads tightly around the space, filling any little holes. Let dry.

3 Cut a slightly smaller circle from a piece of patterned paper and adhere, pattern side up, to the back side of the beaded heart.

jump rings

die-cut border

die cut

For the last 4 years the girls have enjoyed decorating candy house around Christmastime in Mary Pat' class. As cute as the little houses the girls look even cuter stuffing their faces with the sweet deco meant for the houses! 2005

ribbon

rub-ons

die cut

sweet traditio

When you can't find just the right size or style of embellishment, consider making your own! I enjoy using polymer clay, which comes in so many colors and can be blended to create others.

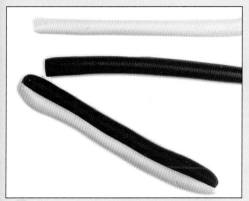

1 Roll white and red clay into separate long logs about ⅛ in. (3mm) thick. Cut the logs into 2-in. (5cm) sections and gently pinch the two colors together.

2 Starting from the middle of the log and working toward each end, slowly twist the colors together.

3 Make a hook on one end of the twisted cane and poke a hole through the top of the hook with a T-pin or paper piercer. Bake clay according to package directions. Let cool. Attach to layout with jump rings.

Tip ✳

When you bake polymer clay like Sculpey, it's good to keep your tools and toaster oven reserved for use only with clay. If you don't want to buy a brand-new toaster oven, check thrift stores for a secondhand bargain.

DON'T STOP THERE...
Did you like playing with clay? Try making candy-corn embellishments with white, orange, and yellow clay. Make a hole in each before you bake them so you can string them on a ribbon, as I did on this treats box.

letter die cuts

Luminous Chihuly

I wanted to echo the translucent beauty of the glass artist's work that is pictured in the photo, so I chose clear buttons and edged them with colors pulled from the art.

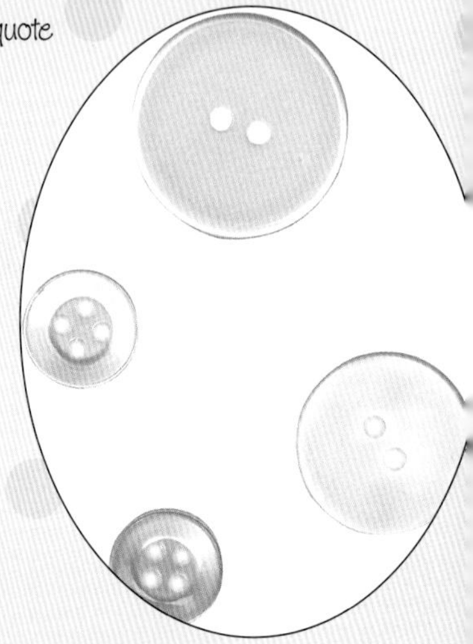

vellum quote

It is not in life, but in art that self-fulfillment is to be found.

George E. Woodberry

1 Choose clear buttons in assorted sizes.

2 Using a brush with a very small tip, paint around the edge of each button. Let dry, then adhere to layout.

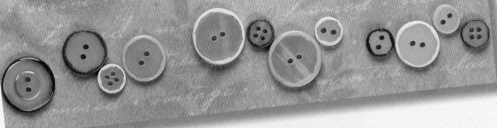

...for the embellishment
- clear buttons
- hobby enamel (various colors)
- small paintbrush

...to make the whole page
- cardstock
- patterned paper
- vellum quote
- letter die cuts
- white gel pen
- adhesive (runner, vellum runner, dots)
- computer

WHAT YOU NEED

time ● ○ ○
expertise ● ○ ○

The dotty theme started with one of the background papers I chose. I carried out a favorite design principle – repetition – by adding sequins to the centers of punched discs.

...for the embellishment
- cardstock (various solid colors)
- circle punch
- small ink pad
- sequins
- tweezers
- adhesive (dots)

WHAT YOU NEED

...to make the whole page
- cardstock
- patterned paper
- letter stickers
- die-cut letters
- wood frame
- letter stamps and ink pad
- ribbon
- rickrack
- embroidery needle
- fiber
- paper piercer or T-pin
- adhesive (runner)
- sewing machine

time ● ● ●
expertise ● ● ○

rickrack

painted wood frame

hand stitching

Claudia

you are like LOUD sunshine and you brighten my world

machine stitching

letter stickers

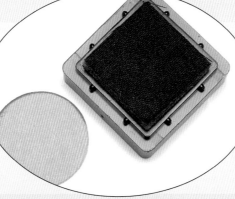

2 Ink edges of circle with a small ink pad.

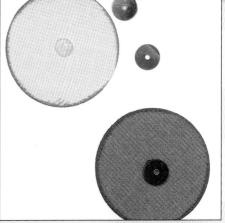

3 Adhere an adhesive dot in the center, then adhere a sequin. Tweezers can help in positioning the sequins.

1 Punch circles from colored cardstock. I used a 1-in. (2.5cm) punch.

beads

new year ANTICIPATION!

"Is it midnight?" "Not yet." "When can we blow our horns?" "At midnight." "Is it midnight?" "No." "Is it time to pop the c
longer do we have to wait?" "Three hours." "Is it midnight in three hours?" "Yes." "Can we scream outside then?" "Yes." "

buttons

rickrack

This page vibrates with all the excitement of a New Year's Eve for kids who get to stay up way past their usual bedtime. You can create shaker boxes in stars or other shapes – whatever fits your theme.

ribbon

1 Trace a large star onto a transparency, white cardstock, and colored cardstock. On the colored cardstock only, trace a smaller star inside the larger star. Cut out all three large stars. Use a craft knife to cut out the smaller star from the larger cardstock star. This will be the frame for the shaker box.

2 Adhere transparency star over the back of the star frame.

3 Trim thin strips of foam adhesive and adhere to the edges of the frame, on top of the transparency star. Sprinkle small beads inside the frame. Peel the backing from the foam adhesive and lay the white cardstock star on top of the foam layer to seal.

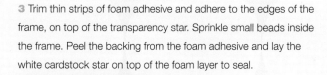

...for the embellishment
- cardstock (white and colored)
- star pattern or template
- fine-tip permanent marker
- transparency film
- craft knife
- seed beads
- adhesive (foam roll or strips)

...to make the whole page
- patterned paper
- ribbon
- rickrack
- buttons
- seed beads
- stickers
- adhesive (runner, strips, dots)
- computer

WHAT YOU NEED

time ●●○
expertise ●○○

DON'T STOP THERE...
This is my Santa's Secret Savings bank! I bought the purse at a craft store and embellished it. Over the photo of Santa is a cutout with a window that holds loose beads – just like the stars on the New Year's page.

2005/2006

ow much hours yet?"

Beaded safety pins

To add dimension, hang tags from safety pins – but don't stop there. Add a row of colorful beads to match the page.

beads paper flowers

...for the embellishment
- rickrack
- safety pin
- seed beads

...to make the whole page
- cardstock
- circle template
- beads
- paper flowers
- acrylic letters
- tweezers
- adhesive (runner, dots)

WHAT YOU NEED

time	●○○
expertise	●○○

1 Overlap two ends of ribbon or rickrack and tie an overhand knot where they cross.

2 Open a safety pin and push the head through the loose part of the knot. Pull knot tight around pin.

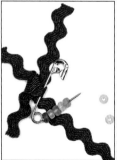

3 Slide beads on tip of pin, leaving room so you can close pin.

DON'T STOP THERE...
I put the same beaded-pin embellishments through the petal cutouts on these little pails, then decorated them for baby shower favors.

metal-rimmed tag

Can you pick out the subtle background embellishment? I added a little dimension with micro beads glued to the berries.

ribbon

machine stitching

Summer Fun!

Berry Pickin'

Wild Raspberries make the best jam, especially when picked with little fingers! Aunt Theresa, Vince, Helen, Claudia, Heidi and Bill   Jump River 2002

...for the embellishment
- patterned paper
- clear glaze
- micro beads
- brayer (optional)

...to make the whole page
- stickers
- ribbon
- metal-rimmed tag
- black marker
- adhesive (runner, dots)
- computer
- sewing machine

time ● ○ ○
expertise ● ○ ○

WHAT YOU NEED

1 Adhere small circles of clear glaze to specific background details (adhesive dots work for this too).

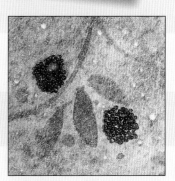

2 Sprinkle micro beads over glue. Gently tap off excess beads and use a brayer or fingers to press beads firmly into adhesive.

Embellishment off the page

I was inspired to create this mini scrapbook-in-a-tin when my daughter found Harry the frog in our backyard. It was the start of an adventure I don't want my kids to forget! Now they have a colorful reminder that they can look at and share anytime. It took a little longer to create than my usual layouts, but it gives focus to each adorable photo so every one can tell a different part of the story. Turn to a mini album like this when you have vacation photos, school photos, or baby's first year.

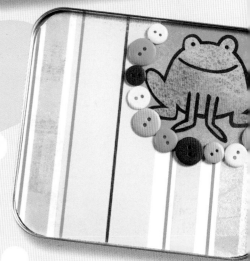

I hope this little project inspires you to take your scrapbook embellishments off the page and into new adventures! All of the techniques I've shared work as embellishment no matter what kind of paper art you're doing — books, cards, collage, and whatever else you love to do.

...to make the whole project

- aluminum tin with mini album
- patterned paper
- frog art
- small sayings
- rub-ons
- letter stickers
- stapler
- ribbon
- rickrack
- buttons
- micro beads
- adhesive, (runner, strips, peel-and-stick sheet, dots, foam squares)

WHAT YOU NEED

time ● ● ●
expertise ● ● ○

THE BEST PART

Edward found Harry in our backyard!

excitement

Isabel was excited to play with Harry.

Harry was very cooperative with the field.

Claudia thought Harry would turn into a handsome prince.

Climbing around the river is fun! Finding the perfect release spot is so important!

favorite summer things

Summer Time

ADVENTURE

The worst part

Freedom! Good bye Harry!

ESCAPE

2005

p. 13

p. 60

p. 70

Use a 6-in. (15cm) square

1

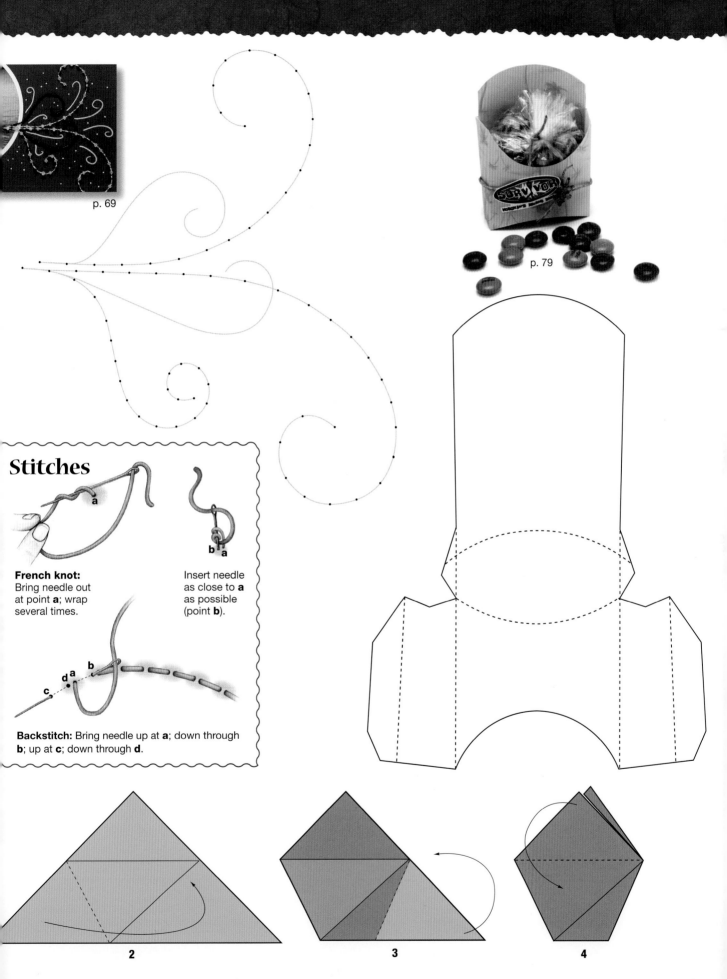

p. 79

Stitches

French knot:
Bring needle out
at point **a**; wrap
several times.

Insert needle
as close to **a**
as possible
(point **b**).

Backstitch: Bring needle up at **a**; down through
b; up at **c**; down through **d**.

2

3

4

Resources

About the author

Heidi Schueller is a contributor to many scrapbooking publications, including Scrapbooking with Beads *and* More Scrapbooking with Beads*, published by Kalmbach Publishing, and was featured as a Memory Makers Master in the book* Scrapbook Embellishments*. A former professional graphic designer, she leads scrapbooking classes nationally and at home in Waukesha, Wis., where she lives with her husband and three children.*

Heidi gives special thanks to her husband for all his support, to the grandmothers for their endless babysitting services, to her children for being patient while mom asks for "just one more," and to friends and family for all their encouragement.

Here is a listing of specific brands used in the scrapbook pages. Keep in mind that product designs change and may no longer be available.

Many of the fonts used can be downloaded free from the Internet; do a search on the font name. Those with "CK" in the name were purchased from Creating Keepsakes.

Spirited fall, p. 8
modeling compound Creative Paperclay
patterned paper Around the Block, My Mind's Eye
cardstock Die Cuts with a View
stickers Chatterbox
rub-on letters, beaded chain Making Memories
lettering template The Crafters Workshop
stamps Lazar Studiowerx

Nauts landing, p. 10
patterned paper Chatterbox, Design Originals
stickers Pebbles Inc.
self-adhesive ink-jet paper Chartpak
font Wade Sans Light

Make a wish, p. 11
patterned paper Die Cuts with a View, My Mind's Eye
ribbon My Mind's Eye
stickers Frances Meyer
chipboard letters Scenic Route
paper flowers Prima
font Toms New Roman

Sisters, p. 12
patterned paper Chatterbox
borders, flower templates Timeless Touches
rub-on letters Making Memories
stamps Hero Arts
font CK Tall Type

Ice cream picnic, p. 13
patterned paper Around the Block
cardstock Die Cuts with a View
stickers Frances Meyer
ribbon Carolace
stamps Lazar Studiowerx
font Whackadoo

100 percent good, p. 14
dog bone pin Around the Block
patterned paper Junkitz
textured cardstock Frances Meyer
large white letter stickers Dural Decal Co.
"good time" letter stickers, stitching rub-ons Die Cuts with a View
small white letter stickers KI Memories

Lucerne, p. 16
patterned paper Die Cuts with a View, Frances Meyer, My Mind's Eye
metal flower beads Cousin Corporation of America

Happy birthday, p. 17
patterned paper Chatterbox
ribbon, rub-ons, circular paper clips, sticker Making Memories
mini pink brads Die Cuts with a View
circular slide mounts Loersch
font Wade Sans Light

Road trip, p. 18
cardstock Chatterbox, My Mind's Eye
round chipboard letters Making Memories
chipboard letters Pressed Petals
flowers Prima
mini yellow brads Die Cuts with a View
fonts Toms New Roman, URW Typewriter Medium

Winter rollercoaster, p. 20
patterned paper My Mind's Eye, Basic Grey
cardstock Die Cuts with a View
letter stickers Chatterbox
stamps Lazar Studiowerx
mini buttons Making Memories

What feeling is so nice, p. 21
patterned paper, ribbon My Mind's Eye
lettering template The Crafters Workshop
chipboard letter Scenic Paper Route
stamps Close to My Heart
mini brads Scrapworks
paper flowers Prima

G&C, p. 22
patterned paper, chipboard Basic Grey
monogram letters, "tough" rub-on My Mind's Eye
ribbon American Crafts
black phone numbers Target
white block stickers KI Memories
"April" rub-on Scenic Route
"&," "are we," "?" rub-ons Making Memories
"zoo" sticker Die Cuts with a View
"2006" stickers, "and" bubble letter stickers Frances Meyer
stamps Close to My Heart

It's not how fast, p. 24
patterned paper Die Cuts with a View (background); DMD and Design Originals (circles)
vellum saying Die Cuts with a View

Swinging, p. 25
patterned paper My Mind's Eye
stickers Chatterbox
chipboard letters Pressed Petals
lettering template The Crafters Workshop

Proud 2B, p. 26
patterned paper, ribbon, chipboard letters, arrow We R Memory Keepers
stitching rub-ons Die Cuts with a View
star spacing template Timeless Touches
stamps Hero Arts
rub-ons Lazar Studiowerx
fonts Wolfe, URW Typewriter

Vegas, p. 28
textured cardstock Frances Meyer
stickers, polka-dot paper Die Cuts with a View

Thanksgiving, p. 29
stickers Die Cuts with a View
number stickers KI Memories
rub-ons StudioWerx
white rub-on number Making Memories
patterned paper Deluxe Designs
clips Provo Craft
brads Magic Scraps
fonts Angelica, Whackadoo, Initial, Briquet, Dream Orphans

True love, p. 30
patterned paper one heart...one mind
jewelry K&Company
white rub-ons Making Memories
black rub-ons Heidi Swapp
font Whackadoo

Man of mystery, p. 32
patterned paper Polar Bear Press
cardstock Die Cuts with a View
stickers doodlebug design inc.
gems Darice
stamp Lazar Studiowerx
UTEE Ranger Industries
Top Boss clear ink Clearsnap

You are my sunshine, p. 33
fabric sticker Making Memories
patterned paper, orange ribbon, buttons Die Cuts with a View
paper flowers Prima
mini gems Darice
glitter glue Ranger Industries

2 little tomboys, p. 34
patterned paper Plaid
fibers, lettering template, tree template Timeless Touches
font CK Twiggy

Boo @ the zoo, p. 36
patterned paper, "THE" stickers Frances Meyer
cardstock Die Cuts with a View
mini brads, "beware" letter stickers Making Memories

Best friends forever, p. 37
colored patterned paper, ribbon We R Memory Keepers
black-and-white patterned paper Die Cuts with a View
stickers Me And My Big Ideas
monogram letters Colorbök

Jack of all trades, p. 38
patterned paper, sayings K&Company
beaded chain Making Memories
stickers Duro Decal
rub-ons Lazar Studiowerx

A season of change, p. 39
cardstock Die Cuts with a View
swirl border punch All Night Media
die-cut leaves Deluxe Designs
small leaf punch EK Success
rub-on words Making Memories

Content being yourself, p. 40
patterned paper Sassafras Lass
fibers, flower stitching template Timeless Touches
wood tag Chatterbox
die-cut letters Sizzix
stamps Provo Craft
lettering template The Crafters Workshop

Naked cowgirl, p. 42
polymer clay Sculpey
patterned paper Die Cuts with a View
fonts Black Widow, Copystruct

Quirky little things, p. 43
patterned paper, "M" letter Scenic Route
large chipboard letter font My Mind's Eye
mini brads The Happy Hammer
letter stickers Die Cuts with a View
rub-ons Lazar Studiowerx
black letter squares Scrapworks
font Wade Sans Light

3 little dears, p. 44
patterned paper My Mind's Eye, Frances Meyer
stamps Lazar StudioWerx
jewels, letter beads Darice
chipboard letters Scenic Route
font FG Adam

T-rex park, p. 46
patterned paper Around the Block
cardstock Die Cuts with a View
letter stamps Stampabilities
dinosaur stamps ANM
font CK Marker

Delightful, p. 47
patterned paper Scenic Route
rub-on word, safety pin Making Memories
font Toms New Roman

Underwater adventures, p. 48
patterned paper Frances Meyer
beaded ribbon Hirschberg Schultz & Co.
die-cut letters Sizzix
stamps Hero Arts

Family portrait, p. 50
patterned paper, snowflake rub-ons My Mind's Eye
"family" rub-ons Heidi Swapp
"portrait" rub-ons Making Memories
snowman stamp Rubber Stampede

Laurelei, p. 51
patterned paper NRN Designs, EK Success
rub-on Making Memories
buckle KI Memories
modeling compound Creative PaperClay
fonts Scriptina, Doodle Cursive

Riverside picnic, p. 52
patterned paper Around the Block, Basic Grey
cardstock S.E.I.
stitching rub-ons Die Cuts with a View
die cuts Sizzix
font Helvetica

Salzburg, p. 54
patterned paper Chatterbox
sparkle flakes Magic Scraps
snowflake die cut Sizzix
fonts Wade Sans Light, Volta T

Beach babes, p. 55
patterned paper Chatterbox
cardstock Die Cuts with a View
die-cut flowers Sizzix
chipboard letters Making Memories
stickers Doodlebug Design

Charming chit-chat, p. 56
patterned paper My Mind's Eye, Scenic Route
letter stickers KI Memories
charms Delight Co.
font SF Happiness

Gram's house, p. 58
patterned paper, cardstock Die Cuts with a View, Flair Designs
chipboard letters, paper flowers Prima
wood tag Chatterbox
rub-on letters Primedia
font CK Journaling

Canine tug-o'-war, p. 59
patterned paper, cardstock, sticker Die Cuts with a View
stickers Making Memories
roll-on transfers Around the Block
lettering template The Crafters Workshop

Goldie locks, p. 60
patterned paper, chipboard Scenic Route
mini brads The Paper Studio
rub-ons Primedia
die-cut letters Sizzix
flower punches EK Success (round), Family Treasures (pointed)
vellum word, mini brads Die Cuts with a View

GG Bob, p. 62
patterned paper, words We R Memory Keepers
stencil letters Chartpak
rub-on decorations Heidi Swapp
rub-on letters Making Memories

Male bonding, p. 63
patterned paper My Mind's Eye and Polar Bear Press
stamps Stampabilities
fish die cut Sizzix
paper clip Making Memories
font Palentino

"B" is for blustery day, p. 64
cardstock Die Cuts with a View
rub-ons, patterned paper Lazar Studiowerx
lettering template The Crafters Workshop
font Susanquill

Locomotive time travel, p. 65
modeling compound Creative Paperclay
patterned paper Flair Designs, Prima
stickers Duro Decal
stamps DSX
fonts President, Ultimatum

Freedom, p. 66
patterned paper Design Originals
silver stars Nicole
ribbon Carolace
lettering template The Crafters Workshop

Kindergarten graduation day, p. 68
patterned paper Flair Designs, Die Cuts with a View
white rub-on letters Making Memories
font Palentino
lyrics Stuart Stott, stuartstott.com

Lake Lucerne, p. 69
patterned paper Around The Block
rub-on letters Making Memories
stickers KI Memories, Doodlebug Design, Duro Decal

Sweet and sour Brian, p. 70
patterned paper, chipboard, adhesive ribbon Die Cuts with a View
"Brian" letter rub-ons Making Memories
stickers Polar Bear Press

10 feet long, p. 71
patterned paper Chatterbox
chipboard letters Scenic Route
rub-ons one heart...one mind

Hodag, p. 72
patterned paper My Mind's Eye, Chatterbox
stamps My Sentiments Exactly
eye candy KI Memories
rub-ons Creating Keepsakes
file tag Creative Imaginations
font Wolfe

Camping frog, p. 74
frog die cut Sizzix
patterned paper Plaid and Junkitz
chipboard letters Pressed Petals
font Foxscript

Nappy bedhead, p. 75
patterned paper Prima, My Mind's Eye
cardstock Die Cuts with a View
stamps Stampabilities
white plastic letters The Paper Studio
"beautiful" letter rub-ons Primedia
"hand-drawn" rub-ons one heart...one mind
font Volta T

Sir Joseph & Sebastian, p. 76
patterned paper one heart...one mind
stamps Close to My Heart

Old World Wisconsin, p. 77
patterned paper Die Cuts with a View and Frances Meyer
cardstock Die Cuts with a View
stickers Chatterbox
font Toms New Roman

Survivor, p. 78
shrink plastic Shrinky Dinks
patterned paper Frances Meyer and Pebbles Inc.
textured cardstock, stickers, ribbon Die Cuts with a View
flower Prima
fonts President, Ultimatum
personalized M&M candies mymms.com

Laughter is the best medicine, p. 80
patterned paper Chatterbox
cardstock, buttons Die Cuts with a View
small rub-ons Heidi Swapp
large rub-ons American Crafts
font Whackadoo

Puppy love, p. 81
patterned paper Chatterbox
stickers, vellum quote, buttons Die Cuts with a View

Sweet tradition, p. 82
polymer clay Sculpey
patterned paper Plaid
ribbon Prima
rub-on letters Making Memories
"tradition" rub-on My Mind's Eye
font CK Tall Type

Luminous Chihuly, p. 84
patterned paper The Crafters Workshop
Short Cuts Brush On Paint Krylon
font Suzannequill

Claudia you are like..., p. 85
patterned paper My Mind's Eye
"Claudia" letter stickers, cardstock Die Cuts with a View
"loud" letters stickers Pebbles Inc.
"world" letter stickers, wood frame Chatterbox
letter stamps Close to My Heart
die-cut letters Sizzix

New year anticipation, p. 86
patterned paper one heart...one mind
green buttons Die Cuts with a View
stickers Colorbök
foam adhesive Scotch

Create, p. 88
cardstock Die Cuts with a View
paper flowers Prima
plastic letters The Paper Studio

Berry pickin', p. 89
patterned paper Provo Craft
stickers Die Cuts with a View
font CK Sloppy

Harry the frog, p. 90
tin with mini album, stitching, "and" rub-ons, letter "H" sticker Die Cuts with a View
frog art Deluxe Designs
patterned paper My Mind's Eye, Chatterbox
small sayings Chatterbox
letter rub-ons Lazar Studiowerx
word rub-ons Scenic Route

Here are the manufacturers of some of my favorite scrapbooking products. They can help you find a retail source for their products.

Around the Block
(801) 593-1946
aroundtheblockproducts.com
cardstock, patterned paper, charms, roll-on transfers

Chatterbox
(208) 461-5077
chatterboxinc.com
cardstock, patterned paper, chipboard, wooden frames

Creating Keepsakes
creatingkeepsakes.com
computer fonts

Creative Paperclay
(800) 899-5952
paperclay.com
air-dry modeling clay

Darice
(866) 432-7423
darice.com
beads, jewels, jewelry-making supplies

Die Cuts with a View
(801) 224-6766
dcwv.com
cardstock, patterned paper, stickers, rub-ons, ribbon

Fiskars
(800) 500-4849
fiskars.com
cutting tools

Frances Meyer/Chartpak
(413) 584-5446
francesmeyer.com
cardstock, patterned paper, stickers, rub-ons, art supplies

JewelCraft
(201) 223-0804
jewelcraft.biz
beads, wire

K&Company
(888) 244-2083
kandcompany.com
cardstock, patterned paper, Frippery jewelry

Krylon
(800) 457-9566
krylon.com
spray paints, spray adhesive, paint pens

Lazar Studiowerx
(866) 478-9379
lazarstudiowerx.com
cardstock, patterned paper, stamps, rub-ons

Making Memories
(801) 294-0430
makingmemories.com
brads, stickers, rub-ons, ribbon

My Mind's Eye
(800) 665-5116
mymindseye.com
cardstock, patterned paper, rub-ons, monograms

one heart...one mind
(913) 681-6745
oneheart-onemind.com
cardstock, patterned paper, ribbon, rub-on words/sayings

Plaid Enterprises
(800) 842-4197
plaidonline.com
cardstock, patterned paper, stamps, acrylic paints, inks

Polyform Products Co.
(847) 427-0020
Sculpey polymer clay

Prima Marketing Inc.
(909) 627-5532
mulberrypaperflowers.com
cardstock, patterned paper, paper flowers

Queen and Co.
(858) 613-7858
queenandcompany.com
beads, accents, charms

Sakura Hobby Craft
(310) 212-7878
sakuracraft.com
Crystal Lacquer

Scenic Route Paper Co.
(801) 542-8071
scenicroutepaper.com
cardstock, patterned paper, chipboard

Sizzix
(877) 355-4766
sizzix.com
die cuts, die-cutting machines

Therm O Web
(847) 520-5200
thermoweb.com
adhesives

Timeless Touches
(623) 362-8285
timelesstouches.net
sewing templates, fibers

Tsukineko Ink
(425) 883-7733
tsukineko.com
inks

We R Memory Keepers
(801) 539-5000
weronthenet.com
cardstock, patterned paper, chipboard, tags